INTEGRATING CULTURE AND OPERATIONS TO...

LiVE
your brand

MICHAEL ARMELI

ENTHUSIASM FOR iBG...

"Outstanding! We started using iBG in August 2013. Their entire business and indeed everyone on their team are enthusiastic—innovative—and totally in sync with the most up-to-date design, establishment and marketing of their client's brand. I can't say enough about their dedication and hard work – and the results achieved. First rate!"

Jim H., President,
Milwaukee Polo Club

"Michael organizes us in creative ways that we haven't thought of."

Todd C., Co-Owner,
Transition Health Benefits

"I have been working with Michael and his company since April, and cannot speak highly enough about their skill, insight and ability to deliver. We are engaged in a full rebranding of my company, and as different hair on fire issues surface, Michael and his crew have been amazing in their ability to turn on a dime and help me resolve them. I believe fully in the value that Michael and his company bring to my organization."

John K., President,
Accenting Chicago Events & Tours, Inc.

"We have been working with iBG for over a year creating our brand from the inside out. They are helping to project our brand to clients and prospects on the outside especially with social media. Equally as important, they are helping our team learn to "live" the brand from the inside. I see great potential for our team to continue to grow and improve as we move forward with iBG."

Jon O., President,
American Advantage Insurance Group

LiVE Your Brand
Author: Michael Armeli
Contributing Author: Amy Oaks
Forward: Samantha Lyn Weber
Editor: Griffin Mill
Cover Design and Interior Layout: Michael Nicloy
Photos and Graphics: integrated Brand Group, Michael Armeli

ISBN: 978-1945907296

BISAC Codes:
BUS 103000 Business & Economics | Organizational Behavior
BUS 097000 Business & Economics | Workplace Culture
BUS 106000 Business & Economics | Mentoring & Coaching

Published by Nico 11 Publishing & Design
www.nico11publishing.com

Be well read.

Quantity order requests can be emailed to:
mike@nico11publishing.com

For more information about
integrated Brand Group, visit:
www.ibrandgrp.com

or scan the QR code below.

iNTEGRATED
BRAND GROUP

To my Sofi . . .
for standing by me
through everything,
EVERYTHING!

LiVE Your Brand...

TABLE OF CONTENTS

Foreword..13

Introduction.....................................17

Sugar...21

Learning My Language.................... 33

Launching iBG.................................41

Change..55

How Does Your Garden Grow..........67

Horses...75

Understanding.................................93

Sugar, Part II...................................103

Letting Go.. 111

Integration.......................................121

Afterword: Last Chance Mustang.....127

About the Authors............................137

FOREWORD
By Samantha Lyn Weber

LIVE Your Brand is much more than just a catchy part of this book's title. It's a philosophy, a way of life, a way of being. Michael Armeli is your field guide through the dense overgrown jungle of business communication, operations, and brand identity. He leads you to a place that you never knew existed, or ever realized could be attained. This is the path that he is expert in carving out for each and every person who has the privilege of partnering with him through integrated Brand Group. When I first began working with Michael at iBG, he shared this wisdom with me, "There are two hurdles to every client relationship: willingness and ability". Many people are willing, but not able to change; or not willing, but know they have the ability to change. A client relationship will not be entirely successful until those two concepts align, and the client is both willing and able to change. Michael shows you the path, and walks it step by step alongside you until together you reach that optimal place for you, your company, and your employees. Once you're there, standards are clear and measurable, and all become fluent in speaking the same language from the inside out, thus LIVING the brand.

I know, because I lived it first-hand. Before I went to work for Michael, he worked with me in a consultant role at another company, where he implemented many of the methods he now continues to use with his clients. This was a broken company at the time, with inefficient systems in place. Much like the Tower of Babel, it seemed a thousand different languages were spoken, and communication between departments was disorganized and unclear. He came in to our department, and from the beginning set the tone that he welcomed my insight, encouraged initiative, and allowed me to make mistakes and learn from them. When I went to work at iBG, the first thing Michael said to me was: "I'm going to ask a lot of you. I'm not kidding, I'm going to ask you for the world. If you can't give it to me, that's okay, but then you have to tell me, 'I can only give you a hemisphere'." Then he flipped it. He said, "And inversely, Samantha, if I ask you for a hemisphere and you're ready to give me the world, you are also responsible for telling me the same." The whole point was to maximize my potential. He sensed—rather, he knew—that I was capable of accomplishing much more than I realized. He demanded responsibility and accountability, but on a path of respect for me as a human being with more limitations on some days than others. It established our working relationship from then on, paving the way for success for us as a team. This is where Michael excels. He is a master at uniting and motivating people, creating and refining language and culture within a company, and seeing the big picture so as to break down and rebuild the smallest detail of operations from the ground up. That might sound like a tall order, but I see it in action every day. I welcome the opportunity to introduce you to Michael and iBG.

Enjoy his story, learn from his models and methods, and discover how to LIVE Your Brand!

INTRODUCTION

Michael Armeli

THE SUITCASE

Remember that phase of your life when everyone asked you, "What do you want to do"? I'm not talking about when you were a child, and everyone asked you what you wanted to be when you grew up. I'm talking about that time later in high school when you were supposed to be seriously thinking about if, and where, you planned to go to college, and what you wanted to do with your life in terms of a career. At first, I used to make something up, so I wouldn't look stupid. I had to at least pretend I had a clue. I knew in my heart at that point though, that I wanted to travel. I wanted to travel and see the world! I wanted to travel, and see the world *with purpose*! I have always been led in this direction, perhaps inspired by visiting family in Italy while growing up, but I have never wanted to see the world as just another tourist. It always needed to have more meaning and depth than that.

So, people would ask me what I wanted to do, and I began to develop a vision in my head. The vision began as a suitcase. This suitcase became more detailed over time, becoming a briefcase-style, brownish-taupe, professional-looking suitcase. This imagery began to illustrate an identity for myself that I couldn't yet put into words. It was my way of beginning to figure out the direction and path I wanted to take, although I didn't yet know what I wanted to BE. Over time, an airplane ticket with the word "Paris" printed on it materialized into the image. More features appeared, fading in and out of the frame as my path became clearer. The picture continued to become increasingly more refined as I figured out what I wanted to do, and where I wanted to do it. Eventually, it sharpened into a close-up picture of myself holding the briefcase and the ticket in the same hand.

I could see the crisp white cuff of a shirt sleeve at my wrist, and the edge of a navy-blue suit sleeve over that. It became a timeline, and it illustrated the evolution of my journey, looking deep within myself to get to know the fire inside.

It's interesting that I did end up traveling extensively in the beginning of my career, and I now metaphorically travel between business cultures every day. That imagery process is very similar to what we do with our operations and identity models, through helping others find their vision, refining it, and putting that vision into practice in the best way possible. And it all started with a suitcase!

SUGAR

*"The past is but the past
of a beginning."*
H. G. Wells

Sugar

FADE IN:

OUTSIDE A FAMILY RESTAURANT - LUNCH TIME
A brown-eyed, dark-haired, six-year-old boy
accompanies his father to the busy Italian
family restaurant they own and run in
Wisconsin.

DISSOLVE TO:

INSIDE THE FAMILY RESTAURANT...DOWNSTAIRS

MICHAEL, the young boy in the scene,
observes the hustle and bustle of the rush,
and the employees doing their various jobs.
He pours himself a soda from the soda gun,
and narrates the scene...

MICHAEL (narrating)
I was downstairs in one of our restaurants
when I realized I was finally tall enough to
reach the soda gun, pour myself a soda, and
stash all the saltine crackers. This was
a monumental day in my life, since I had
been tagging along to the restaurant with
my parents for as long as I could remember.

I was standing on my tip-toes stretched up as tall as I could to get that soda gun, when I suddenly noticed this WAITRESS, who I thought was old at the time, but was probably only in her early twenties. Her name was Kim, and she was MEAN! She was this blonde girl, and *everyone* feared her… or at least *I* feared her. My eyes grew wide as I watched her hastily grab a handful of sugar packets, and jam them fiercely into the containers. Wow, did she look scary doing that! I asked her,

MICHAEL
"Why are you doing that like that?"

She snapped her head around at me with an angry expression on her face and shouted,

WAITRESS
"WHAT?!"

MICHAEL (narrating)
I was petrified, and dashed upstairs to my Dad's office, where I sat quietly and waited until it was time to go home.

CUT TO…

IN THE CAR ON THE WAY HOME:

MICHAEL (narrating)
I continued my silence in the car on the way home until my dad asked,

DAD
"What's the matter?
Is everything all right?"

MICHAEL
"How do you fill the sugar containers?"

(narrating)
I was only six years old, and that was the
only way I knew how to ask this very, very
complex question in my head. It was the
only way I could get it out.

DAD
"What do you mean?"

MICHAEL (narrating)
My dad couldn't understand a simple
question like that.
He asked me three times,

DAD
"What do you mean?!"

MICHAEL (narrating)
I repeated three times,

MICHAEL
"Well…how do you fill the sugar containers?"

MICHAEL (narrating)
I didn't want to get into it that the mean
waitress yelled at me like an angry psycho,
because I couldn't express all that. After
our exchange of the same question and
answer three times, it didn't go very well
in the car, and then it got worse and my
Dad was MAD. I couldn't WAIT to get home.

CUT TO...

HOME:

My dad yelled for my mom...

                    DAD
                  "MARIE!!"

Mom rushes out of the house, running toward us

                    MOM
              "What? What?!"

                    DAD
     "YOUR SON! He's been asking me like
   three or four times how to fill the sugar
                containers!!"

            MICHAEL (narrating)
   My Mom looked at me, as I stood there in
   my continuing silence, still as a statue.
   She looked at my dad, and he stood there
   frustrated, waiting for her response. She
     looked back at my dad expectantly and
                  inquired,

                    MOM
     "Well Joe...how do you fill the sugar
                containers?"

            MICHAEL (narrating)
        And he... just... LOST it!!

                    DAD
           "GODDAMNSONOFABITCH!!"

DISSOLVE TO…

BACK AT THE RESTAURANT THE NEXT DAY:

MICHAEL (narrating)
The next day I went back to the restaurant with my mother, and I followed her around closely because I was worried the mean waitress was there. I noticed my mother pick up a tray, and gently set it on a table. She gathered a linen napkin and placed it perfectly in the center of the tray. She chose a sugar container, and she carefully counted out the sugars; seven white, six pink, four blue. She lined them all up in an orderly fashion, facing the same way. Next, she typed the process into a document on the computer, and printed it out. It said "Sugar Container Procedure". She taped it to the wall, and put the tray with the napkin and sugar on it as a display, like that day's version of a power point. She just did it. She didn't explain it to me that day, or say anything further about it later, but she knew I was right there with her, watching her do it all.

FADE TO BLACK…

I didn't know at that time that I'd just done my first case study in real life. I was already, at that young age, acutely aware that angrily stuffing the sugar containers was not a fit with the culture my parents had created in their restaurant. That waitress's body language and tone of voice were not the language spoken there! I went on to work in a variety of roles as I grew up in the restaurant business. Although the hospitality industry wasn't to be my ultimate career path, it was the perfect classroom for a variety of lessons that shaped me, and the "brand" that I became. It molded my work ethic, the way I think, how I analyze a situation or organization, the way I relate to and treat people. It's almost impossible to set your beginnings aside and say they aren't a part of who you are. Only when we recognize and embrace the past, can we move forward to become who we are meant to be—both as a person and as an organization.

Looking back at growing up in the restaurant and hospitality business, it was not just the way my parents made a living...It was *the way we lived.* I began by going along to work with my parents and simply being there with them and my older brothers. I played on the adding machine, watched them work, and eventually began to help with the little things like counting money. I could help with simple tasks in the office, and felt like I was a part of the team and a valued part of the family. Once I could hold a tray, I would run around with the tray and pretend to be a waiter.

I'm sure at the time, my parents just needed to keep me out of the way and occupied, but it set up a natural progression of learning and gained responsibility. The lessons learned were interwoven naturally into these experiences.

> *Only when we recognize and embrace the past, can we move forward to become who we are meant to be - both as a person and as an organization.*

FIVE LESSONS LEARNED IN
THE RESTAURANT BUSINESS:

1. Take Care of Business First
… In the Office

The reality is that restaurants aren't just about food and presentation. Yes, without food there is no restaurant, but there is a front end of the restaurant and then a whole behind-the-scenes piece that makes up the backbone of the organization. I started observing behind the scenes going to work with my parents at a very young age, so I learned that there was a lot of work that went into running the business side of a restaurant before any magic could even begin to happen in the kitchen.

2. The Importance of First Impressions
…Hosting

We all know about the importance of first impressions. It didn't matter how busy we were; the role of the host or hostess was to welcome, and bring order to the chaos of seating in an ever-changing scene of customers!

3. Attention to Detail
…Bussing

The most poignant lesson I learned as a busser was if you didn't have something in your hands each time you went into the kitchen, you weren't doing your job. If you looked around, there was always something to pick up.

4. Keep Cool Under Pressure
…Serving and Bartending

These skills applied to many roles in the restaurant business, but, I learned the most during the rush between 5:00 and 8:00pm. I navigated how to talk to people, handle a crisis, multi-task, and make it look good in front of customers. I learned from my mistakes instantly, in real-time, so it was very impactful.

5. Be Willing to do Whatever Needs to be Done
…Playing all of the Roles

Throughout the years that my family owned restaurants, I washed dishes, bussed, cooked, waited tables, hosted, bartended...I did everything! I knew that business inside and out because of the many roles I played.

LEARNING MY LANGUAGE

*"I said do you speaka my
language? He just smiled and
gave me a vegemite sandwich."*

*Colin Hay
and Ron Strykert*

After a typical high school experience, I left Wisconsin for the warmer weather of Arizona, and college. I enjoyed the college scene, and the laid-back Arizona lifestyle. I spent the first three years taking the requisite breadth-requirement classes for a degree, along with an assortment of foreign language classes. By my junior year, I still didn't know what I wanted to major in, much less what I wanted to do with my life after college. One day, my mom called to see how I was doing. I replied, "Good. I got all B's and a couple of C's."

She paused, and then said, "You know, your Dad has to push out a lot of pizzas for you to get just a C." Her timing was perfect, and her words hit me right in the gut. I hadn't applied myself to the best of my abilities to that point, and my parents had been paying for my mediocrity.

I went to my guidance counselor the very next day, feeling beside myself and lost. I told her, "I don't know what I want to do...And I don't know if what I'm doing now is working."

We had an extensive discussion, and I finally confessed to her, "These are the classes I do well in, these are the classes I don't do well in, and this is why."

I continued to hone in on my strengths without even realizing that I was promoting them. I was coming to the realization that I excelled in, and loved, foreign language classes.

I asked her, "Can I just take all foreign language classes

and graduate?" I figured there were plenty of related opportunities that I'd love to experience out in the world; I could be a teacher, interpreter, or work for the United Nations. Plus, I figured at least I'd get all A's for sure!

She informed me, "No, you can't."

So I left that meeting, and promptly set up another meeting with a different guidance counselor. I posed the same question, "Can I just take all foreign languages and graduate?"

This particular guidance counselor replied, "Well that's interesting. If you write up a curriculum, the Dean will look it over and we'll see."

> Take a strength, skill set, or passion, and then blend that with other aspects of what you do, whether in school, business or life. Integration is the key to maximizing them.

I spent some time after that writing up a curriculum (or what I thought was a curriculum). I had already passed all the phonetics, linguistics, literature, and cultural aspects for French, Spanish, and Italian. I had all the basics for these languages down and then some. In order for my curriculum to stand a chance for approval, I needed to take my language major concept, and then make that discipline *inter-disciplined* with the business classes. This is the crux of the integration concept we use every day at iBG: take a strength, skill set, or passion, and then blend that with other aspects of what you do, whether in school, business or life. Integration is the key to maximizing them.

I presented my curriculum to the Dean, and pitched, "I'm not in the business school because I'm not smart enough, or I didn't apply myself as well as I could have, but I bet I can take all your business classes in each of these languages."

The Dean approved my curriculum, and I charged ahead through the rest of my degree that way. I took Economics, Marketing, and the rest of the business classes I needed to graduate under the umbrella of each of the languages for those courses. We created a new "Interdisciplinary Degree", which included majors and minors in French, Spanish, and Italian.

I had finally found my niche.

Following graduation, I took a job as an interpreter with the tourism bureau in St. Petersburg, Florida. I flew in, and worked for about two weeks before Hurricane Charley hit, and I was evacuated. On the way to Atlanta out of St. Petersburg, an international company based out of Milwaukee, Wisconsin, called and offered me a position as a "Brand Liaison". The position was really a glorified interpreter for them in Europe, but I took that job on the spot, excited to be based in Zurich, Switzerland. Once I arrived in Zurich, I realized there was so much more to language than speaking it verbally. It's about:

- Here's how we act
- Here's how we dress
- Here's how we maintain our desk space
- Here's how we maintain our bathrooms
- Here's our phone etiquette

There's a whole culture and system behind the words that we speak. It works in different ethnic cultures, and it works in business in corporate culture. When you go to another country, you might fly in, land, read signs, and talk to get your bearings and figure out what to do next. What if you don't speak the language? It's much tougher to communicate; complicated by the fact that if you aren't familiar with the culture, you might also be confused by the non-verbal signals sent your way. For example, when you fly in to Italy and enter the airport, you immediately see attractive women wearing official police uniforms accessorized with high heels and Dolce & Gabana handbags. They look at you—and they know you look lost and need help—but they don't approach you or offer assistance until you ask them. We as Americans might consider that rude, but that's just their culture. They're waiting. Their culture is not necessarily to approach, but to be approached. They use their hands actively when they speak, and we might think they're getting all in our space, but that's their language. They can make a bunch of gestures and, without speaking a word, "say" quite a bit that way.

Now imagine your first day on the job in a corporate environment. You walk into the office and land at your desk, or cubicle. Maybe you were on-boarded, and acclimated to company policies and procedures; but in most companies, that still doesn't clue you in to all the unspoken rules of that department within the company, and overall corporate culture. You still must navigate your way through how to read, speak, and LIVE the brand of your new company. All too often, the on-boarding process is incomplete, not followed through, or doesn't happen at all. In these cases, you might have to find your own way to communicate, and possibly make decisions that end up being toxic, and hurting you or the organization over time. A good on-boarding and training process will teach you to automatically respond to situations from the point of view of the brand, without even having to think about it. In the same way, it's said that you're fluent in a language when you think and speak in the language, without having to translate it in your head.

Culture is Complicated!

Prior to moving to Zurich, I learned about the company, the people there, the office, and the culture of the country. After I settled in, I began to immerse myself into the culture of that specific office within the company. It soon became apparent that there was a general disdain by that location for corporate headquarters, compounded by the fact that it was in the United States. Yes, technically Europe and the United States are friends. We all get along for the most part, and successfully conduct quite a bit of diplomatic and commercial business with one another. But, at that time with that group of people, there was also a strong undercurrent of dislike for the Americans, creating significant segregation between the Zurich location and the United States location. It manifested itself culturally through the way the Europeans were treated when they traveled to the United States for meetings, versus how they would treat the Americans when they came to Zurich. I would hear, "When we go to the U.S., we have to catch a cab and figure out where we need to go. Then they take us out to a cheap restaurant to eat. When they come over here, we pick them up at the airport and take them to their hotel. We have them in to our homes for dinner, and take them out for coffee."

I quickly learned about those cultural differences in how people are treated, how important it is to integrate cultures within an international company's locations, and to define the standard by which you expect to be treated. That not only applies to companies with locations in multiple countries, but also to companies with locations in multiple domestic markets. Even within the United States, different states abide by different etiquette standards, which can then vary between individual cities within those states.

Beyond differences between the two countries, brand strategies developed by the American teams never seemed to translate well to the European market. There was always a huge difference of opinion in terms of the strategies themselves, how they were designed, and when they were to be deployed. In addition, these strategies were rolled out with little training or involvement from individual markets to build buy-in and successful implementation. The ongoing struggle and strife between the two international locations fascinated me. I saw it as a problem that permeated deeply inside the culture within the company. The larger problem was how poorly that defective culture was married with how they operated. When that marriage isn't good, you don't have a very good deliverable, and you don't have a good foundation on which to build success.

During my three years with that company, I realized there was also a disconnect between our customers and our offices, and that we needed to figure out a way to better harmonize the two. I created a system to remedy the problem, and presented it to upper management. I was essentially told, "It's not going to change, and if you stay here, you'll burn out. It's too toxic." I left the company soon after that. They did me a huge favor by giving me that advice. Leaving that position set me free to develop and refine the systems of, and continue to build upon the concept of improving company culture and branding through language models. It was a risk, and it wasn't easy, but I was able to jump right into consulting with both feet, and begin my next career adventure.

LAUNCHING iBG

*"Living at risk is jumping off
the cliff and building your wings
on the way down."*

Ray Bradbury

I settled back in the United States with the brand identity and operations models I had created in Zurich perfected, and ready to go. Those models were inspired by how we learn and become fluent in a language, and the organizational dysfunction I observed while working in Zurich. I knew there had to be a way to get everyone on the same page; all speaking the same company language and working toward common goals. Looking at how we learn how to speak a language, we start with:

- Learning letters (an alphabet)
- Building words
- Constructing sentences
- Reading it
- Writing it
- Speaking it
- LIVING it (Fluency)

It's said that we're not actually fluent until we dream in that language; in other words, when it becomes automatic and we don't have to translate it in our heads before speaking it. That's how living your brand should be. It's the difference between saying, "I sell insurance" and "I protect people's property". They each describe what you do, but which sentence sounds more intriguing? Which shows that you're living your brand?

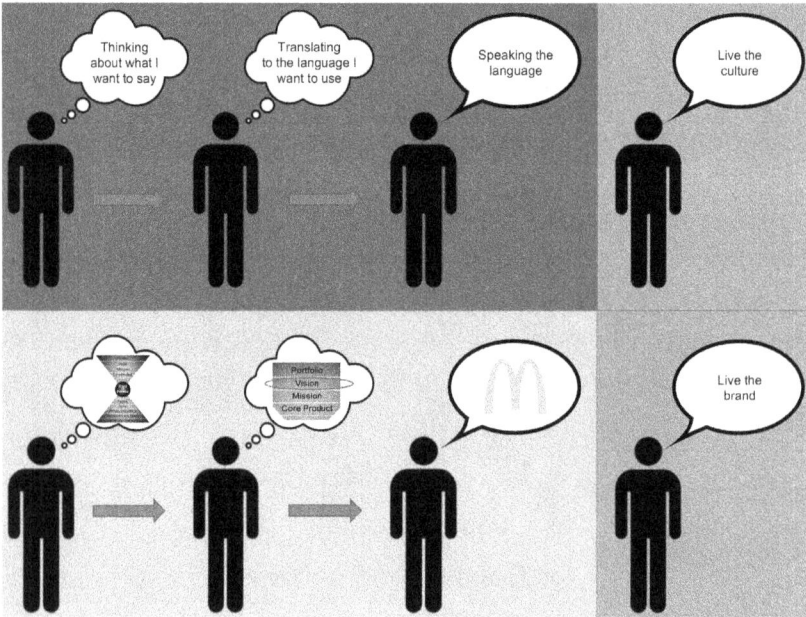

I set out to change the world through brand integration; that is marrying the identity of a company with well-defined operations to create success. First and most importantly, the entire organization of a company from the lowest-ranked employees all the way up to the CEO must be clear on exactly who they are collectively, and how their individual roles fit into that vision. It begins with language and culture. Remember a time when you began a new job. You probably received an employee manual. That manual likely highlighted the company mission statement, and should have included Standard Operating Procedures (SOP) for a variety of situations pertaining to your job. That's great. It seems logical that those two pieces of information would provide a road map for "how to be" within that company, right? However, I realized early on that memorizing a company mission statement doesn't necessarily teach you how to incorporate those ideals into the daily routine of doing your job. They are merely words that imply different meaning to different people depending on their own interpretations and past experiences. The value behind that mission statement, and what those words mean within the context of the company are what's most important.

Memorizing a company mission statement doesn't necessarily teach you how to incorporate those ideals into the daily routine of doing your job.

We could apply this same philosophy to "elevator pitches". Don't waste your time building one singular response to the question, "What do you do?" Ideally, an elevator pitch forms organically depending on who you're speaking with, and the context of the question. If you're fluent in your company language and culture, that's easy. You have no translating to do. Your answer will differ depending on if the person asking is a potential customer, or perhaps a competitor. It will differ based upon how much knowledge that person has of your business, and the industry you work within. You might answer differently if you are waiting in line somewhere making casual conversation, or at an industry conference. You want to connect to the person you're speaking with in each situation, but that's not going to happen if you're using one canned elevator pitch. It's important to be able to live your brand by speaking the language, and embodying the culture effortlessly.

We use the "Identity Model" to develop the language within a business culture when working with a client on brand identity. It could involve building a language from scratch, or fortifying the existing language to clean it up and fine-tune it.

We begin with this visual of a funnel:

Brand Strategy: Identity Exhibit

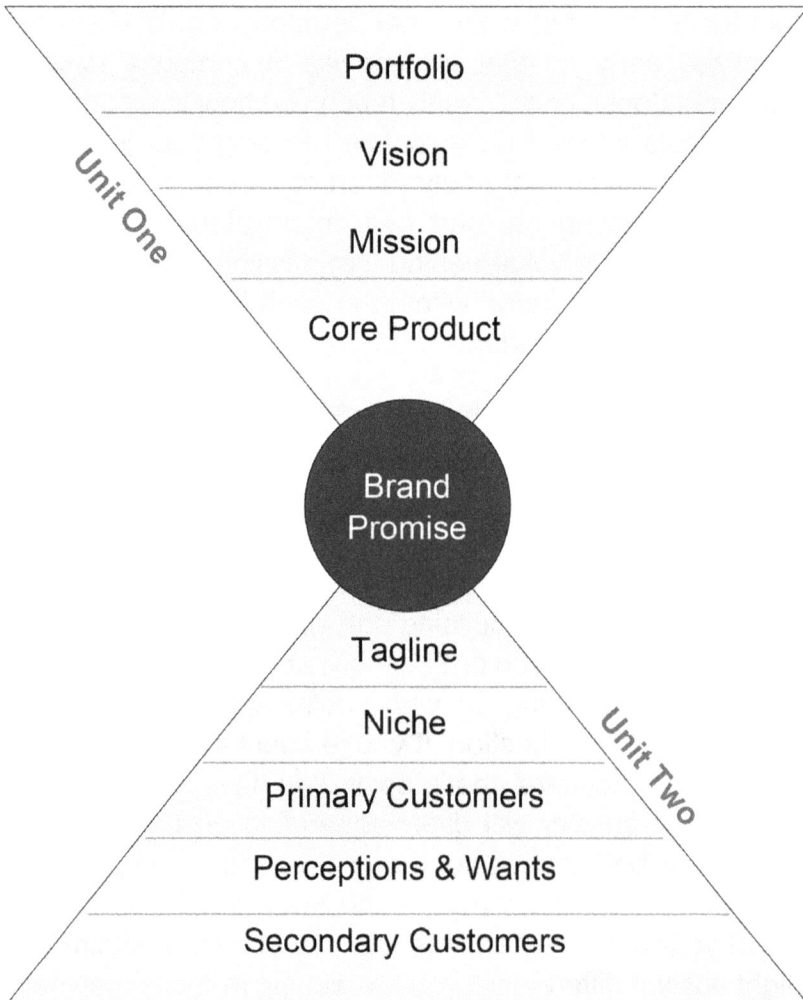

The funnel represents <u>levels of engagement</u> in communication. The widest part of the funnel at the very top captures everything. Imagine that it's raining, and you're thirsty. You need water to drink, so you gather as much of that nourishing rainwater as you can into your funnel. After you collect the rainwater, it will go through several layers of filters and purification before you can drink it. The same applies to communication. We want to appeal to as many people as possible at that top level of engagement to entice them, and spark interest in what we have to say. But it doesn't stop there. Once we have their attention, we carry on with our story, keep telling it, making it more interesting and detailed as time goes on. Some of these people will fall out, and some of these people will travel with you until you've cascaded all the way down to the bottom of the funnel. It is here that we find the most concise clarity in the message we wish to convey.

The journey to the bottom of the funnel is not as straight-forward as simply falling through to the end. Within each level of engagement, we run our interactions through filters to consider factors like:

- Are they acutely attuned and interested?
- Are they bored?
- Are they paying attention?
- Are they distracted?

When talking with someone in any language, it's important to pay attention and notice if he or she is engaged, and at what level. At the end of the day, we can use these levels of engagement to maximize the conversation. Breaking it down further, each level represents a crucial piece of this puzzle.

UNIT ONE

PORTFOLIO: What do you do?

If iBG is working with "Acme" Corporation, and they are our client, I ask the people in the company who I'm working with the simple question, "What does Acme Corporation do?" That should elicit a collective conversation about what Acme Corporation is and does. We keep the conversation moving, and facilitate deeper thinking from that place. Ideally, we want them to come up with an answer to the question "What does Acme Corporation do?" that prompts a follow-up question from the person they are engaging. It's about so much more than just what the company *does*. It's defining that concept into a PORTFOLIO of what that business is and does in a very creative, intriguing, and specific way. For example, we could say we are a high-quality company, but what does that mean? The concept of quality differs from business to business. The quality we expect from McDonald's is quite different from the quality we expect from Starbucks. If we use the word "quality", we need to define that term specific to our business, then re-invent the language and use those terms. If we are successful in doing this, we will take them to the next level of engagement, or:

VISION: What do you strive for?

The definition of a vision is something you continuously work toward, but never attain. If you do reach your vision, it wasn't very well defined in the first place! Think of your vision as an unattainable goal, not in a futile way, but in a positive light. When you're striving for your vision, you are forever aiming to be your best. When you come close to reaching your vision, it's time to enhance it, raising the bar ever higher.

> When you're striving for your vision,
> you are forever aiming to be your best.

MISSION: What are the steps you take in reaching toward your vision?

Your Mission is the *what* that you do, but more specifically a categorical summation of these steps, propelling you toward your vision without quite reaching it. We ask the question, "What's your daily routine at work?" Some people are very specific, listing each task. Others categorize those tasks into a group. We combine lists, and end up with a very detailed mission listing all the tasks together underneath their respective categories. We begin to see the intangible becoming tangible at this stage of the model, and it leads to the most challenging piece:

CORE PRODUCT:
How do you do *what* you do every day?

This is the hardest part to grasp. When people are immersed in how they're doing what they're doing, they can't express it. We lead them through that process by listening, turning what they've said around to tell them "how", allowing them to respond, telling them "how" again…over and over until there's no more ability to ask the question "how" any longer. That might sound tedious, but it's a very collective process. This piece will bring a room together–even if they can't stand one another. It's extremely transformational and a lot of fun! The Core Product piece of the model is enlightening on many levels, and leads the group just short of the question "Why do we do things this way?"

BRAND PROMISE: What do you promise?

The Brand Promise essentially restates the process, and summarizes it. What exactly is it that you promise? That sounds like a deep question—and it is—but we've given the client the tools to answer it through the previous steps completed in the Identity Model. We begin to guide the group toward an answer by asking everyone to review the levels of engagement, and then write down one thing from each level that resonated the loudest for them. That could be a term that has already been defined, or it could be a thought associated with a concept we discussed. Each person ultimately takes each of these things, meshes them together, and then tells me what they promise. Inevitably, each of these individual promises from each individual person ends up being quite similar, yet not quite the same. Each person needs to be able to comfortably convey the brand promise in his or her own words, communicating passion and feeling about the brand. When that happens, they are speaking the company language, and no longer simply memorizing and reciting a "Mission Statement". We can morph these individual Brand Promises to create one collective Brand Promise, but also allow and encourage the freedom of each person to share that story in his or her own compelling way. It's an amazing process to facilitate, and very rewarding to watch the transformation take place.

UNIT TWO

TAGLINE: Brainstorm Drop Tank

Unit Two is all about tangibility, differentiation, and plain facts. They are very engaged at this point, learning the language, and we at iBG need to keep that momentum going. We want them to be fluent in their company language: go out into the world and speak it! This part of the process begins with brainstorming a Tagline. When anyone comes up with a brilliant brainstorm at any time throughout the learning process, we drop it into the Tagline section, and set it aside for later. It's important to note that there is no one perfect tagline for any company, so it's good to have a collection of them at the ready.

NICHE: Why should someone choose to work with you over anyone else?

The most unique thing about any culture is its people, so we steer the conversation into what makes them special as individuals. We get them talking about themselves. The process becomes possessive and personalized. I like to use the analogy that you don't put your kids into every activity on the planet. They might start with several to sample different things, but eventually they find their talents and passions, and focus on activities that cultivate those. The same applies to business and brand. *What about you and your company sets you apart from the rest?*

PRIMARY CUSTOMERS: Who is on your current customer list?

These are the people who know you so well, and they put your business at the forefront of their consciousness so much, that they contact you and nobody else when they have a need. We collectively describe and define Primary Customers in two different ways: Who is that category of customer, and what are they like? Are they men or women? Are they wealthy or lower income? Are they strong or are they struggling? We clarify that so it's very clear who makes up their client base.

PERCEPTIONS & WANTS: Pride in the culture, and conveying how you want to be perceived.

This stage is all about re-invigorating the culture as a reminder to the employees that they own it! Owning it means understanding that they must tell the world how they wish to be perceived, rather than allowing the world to perceive them, and then accepting that judgment. Another way to look at it is asking the question, "What do you want your customers to want?" Often when business is good, we default to giving our customers anything they want and think they need. But the relationship likely began with giving the customers what you wanted them to want; creating a need. I'll often illustrate this by playing a national anthem. Sometimes it's the national anthem of the United States, but other times I'll play the Italian or French national anthem and transpose the words into English for all to see and understand. National anthems naturally impart a sense of honor and pride both by their lyrics, and through the act of singing them. We come together as a nation, and feel close and strong when singing together in a group. National anthems cultivate unwavering ideals, and remind us about who we are as a country. Similarly, I'll illustrate that point using myself as an example, showing how I respond when someone says (usually with a sense of disdain), "Oh, so you're a *consultant*". THAT gets my dander up! I am NOT just a consultant, and who are you to tell me who I am? It immediately invigorates the audience to get involved and contribute corrections. They learn that if you correct someone politely, gracefully, and stunningly, it leaves an indelible mark on that person's conscience. That person will never forget who you are or what you do, and when asked about you, he or she will say something exciting. It might be positive or it might be negative, but it won't be boring! This level of engagement is my personal favorite because so many people fumble around here, and that fumbling elicits a fantastic learning opportunity. For example, if someone asks you, "Are you an accountant?" and you reply, "Yes." Think about what you just did to your company; you made it completely obsolete. Think about different nationalities, and the people who are innately proud to be of a certain heritage. That pride emanates from deep within their very being, and permeates every thought, word, and deed in some way. That is the kind of self-confidence in brand identity and language we're looking to cultivate within a business.

If you correct someone politely, gracefully, and stunningly it leaves an indelible mark on that person's conscience.

SECONDARY CUSTOMERS: The Future

The final level of engagement is crucial to perpetuating the business. If you forget about your secondary customer, you might as well close up shop. Your secondary customers are those who don't use you today, but might use you tomorrow. They are the referrals, and the next generation of primary customers. McDonald's does a great job of constantly looking for the next generation of customers. Not only do they offer salads for the health-conscious customer, but Happy Meals for the youngest kids coming into the restaurant with their caregivers. The McDonald's brand is in front of those kids constantly, growing them up into their regular adult consumers-to-be.

Even when you become fluent in a language, mindfulness in communication is still crucial. I have learned that through visiting family in Italy. Although I'm fluent in *their* native tongue (Italian), there's an additional level of effort put into the conversation because it isn't in *my* native tongue (English).

I remember traveling to Italy in my late teens and early twenties. I could communicate just fine—both speaking and listening—but I remember feeling exhausted after some conversations. Looking back, that exhaustion resulted from putting intense amounts of effort into making sure they understood what I was saying. My family over there is very special to me. I would have deep discussions with my cousins about family members we'd lost, or situations in life we were working through. I worried that my message wasn't being relayed accurately because I might not know the exact word, or dialect variation. I felt such an intense bond with my family after those conversations. The intensity of that bond is truly remarkable when you put energy and purpose into communication. I don't think it's any different when you have an intense conversation in your native tongue. It's just easier to speak, and you're not so focused on making sure the words you've spoken are understood. Taking that further, it's no different when speaking and living your brand. When someone doesn't recognize a brand, or isn't very familiar with it, then the words about it don't mean much in the beginning. Once that client, or potential client, becomes more familiar with the brand, there should be more effort and depth put forth into that conversation. The message is more than just words, but also includes personalization, and authentically shows the meaning underneath it all.

CHANGE

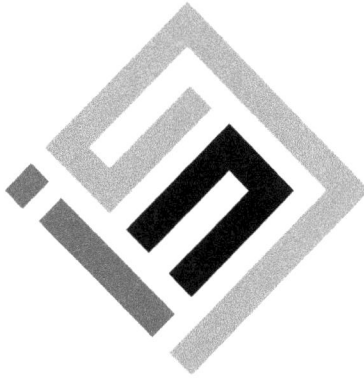

"There is nothing more difficult to take in hand, more perilous to conduct, or more uncertain in its success, than to take the lead in the introduction of a new order of things."

Niccolo Machiavelli

I love that one of our first clients ever at iBG was a realist. Betty worked with an organization that provided day care for mentally ill and developmentally disabled children and adolescents. Her famous phrase was, "What can go wrong will go wrong". What can go wrong with mentally ill or developmentally disabled children and adolescents, the staff that served them, and the houses that housed them, absolutely will go wrong. That's why they always had to be beyond prepared for the situations they hadn't thought of yet, but that definitely would happen at some point in time.

- That's why standards are so important.
- That's why language is so important.
- That's why standards + language = success

With this client, we needed to implement precise language, and processes, that would guide staff to respond to any possible scenario in the best way possible, authentically representing the brand and the message. We needed to be able to give direction clearly and precisely to a staff member, and know that he or she could then infer anything else that might be subjective. For example, if an employee was told to "make the place look good", twenty very different, low-paid, under-skilled caregivers could interpret that in twenty different ways. The definition of "good" varies. Good could mean the doors are open, but not clean. Are the blinds open or closed? Is the room dusted or just decluttered? Betty took me fully into their culture, immersed me, and helped me develop a very good campaign to bring to life what their organization was trying so hard to bring to the community.

When I visited Betty's facility for the first time, she brought me into a room knowing I had no idea what I was walking into. This room, located far inside the building, had no windows, and was filled with patients and their care-givers at a 1:1 ratio. The door opened, I walked in, and all activity going on prior to my arrival completely stopped. Everyone stared at me, the foreign object in the room. I could feel their prying eyes asking, "Who is that?" and "What is this about?" Almost instantly, one child stood up and fell to the floor. His caregiver didn't catch him soon enough, so she simply picked him up off the floor, and sat him back in his chair. He sustained a scrape on his body, and I could see he was bleeding. I just stood there. Once again, he tried to stand up, and leaned forward, but this time his caregiver caught him and sat him back in his chair. He did it a third time, and his caregiver finally secured him with a seatbelt. After I left the room that day, Betty and I had a major discussion.

I said, "OK so here's what I saw today…You realize that none of it matches up with what your brand identity says about you?"

Betty was very receptive. She was completely open to learning, when many others were not.

I asked, "Why did that child continue to do the same thing? It didn't seem like he cared about getting hurt?"

She responded, "Because that was his way of getting from point A to point B, and he wanted to come to you."

I then asked what seemed obvious to me, "Why didn't anybody bring me to him, instead of having to restrain him with a seatbelt?"

This was not a dangerous criminal who doesn't get second chances. This was a developmentally disabled child who couldn't maneuver himself, so that was his failed attempt at maneuvering.

Betty responded honestly, "We cannot have incidents on our incident report. If we have incidents on our incident report, we will get cited and shut down."

I asked, "Is that your primary goal? You want to be proactive, and expand horizons for these consumers, providing them a safe, comfortable environment. It looks to me like you're operating from a more defensive stance. Can't you have chairs with wheels, and allow that child to move himself?"

Consequently, several months later they did exactly that. We worked together to implement change, and that child had zero incidents for five months, which was a huge success! That's killing two birds with one stone; keeping clients safe while striving for a greater vision.

This business operated facilities all over the country, and were clients of iBG for about four years. They struggled early on, with quite a few facilities running at far less than capacity. To begin, we collaborated internally through the Identity Model, and by standardizing operating procedures. We made sure employees were living the culture—and those standards—before executing an outside marketing campaign. As a result of the campaign, we filled two facilities in Milwaukee alone within three months. We worked on another day treatment facility with room for forty patients and filled that facility.

The success came from being able to say they deliver consistent, high quality affordable care; and proving it. Placement specialists look at facilities, and want to see that Standard Operating Procedures are in place and successfully implemented. They look at employee evaluations and other elements of quality control. They only place patients in facilities that they trust, and that trust comes from knowing that the product can be delivered.

The process we navigated with Betty's company illustrates the point that speaking the language and living the culture is a strong beginning, but it's also crucial that an organization knows how to *optimally function*. It's not enough to portray yourself fluently and authentically on behalf of the company; what does everyone in the organization *do* with that behind the scenes? It's only through pairing well-defined operations—that is, clear and concise procedures along with clear and concise standards—that an organization can truly thrive. This was the key for Betty and her day care facilities. Operations and standards needed a complete overhaul before we could even think about marketing and filling up those facilities.

At iBG, we are about breaking things down to authentic true form, and then rebuilding from the ground up based off of that authenticity. The Diamond Exhibit perfectly illustrates how we make this happen:

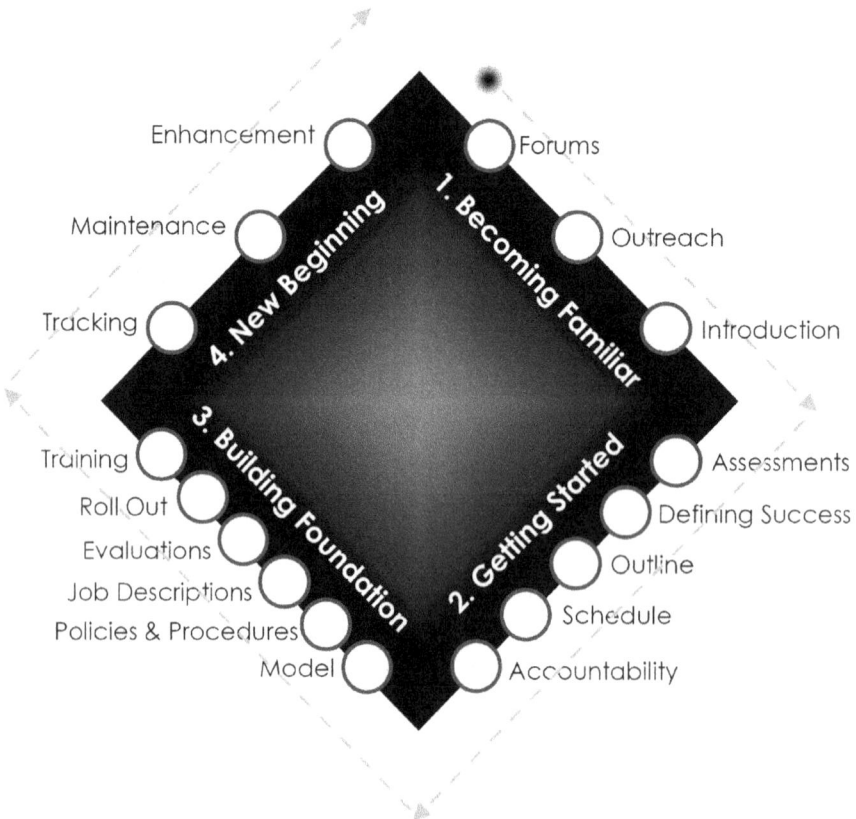

Starting from the center of the diamond, we break it down into four broad steps:

Becoming Familiar

iBG has to get to know the business and the people within the business, and they have to get to know us. Without trust and familiarity, change will be nearly impossible to implement.

Getting Started

Think of this as the research phase. We must determine where current standards and procedures lie, in order to know where to begin. We look at how each person accomplishes tasks and reaches objectives. Do they even know what their objectives are? Are they well-defined? Some businesses already operate within clear parameters, and others function in a much more intuitive and ambiguous way. iBG evaluates the organization, and determines whether we need to build in new structure from the bottom up, or tweak the existing system already in place. Any dysfunction within the organization usually becomes apparent during this part of the process. We also begin mapping out the steps we'll follow toward new standards and success.

Building Foundation

Just as the name implies, this stage constructs the framework on which to build steps toward improvement and continued success. Together, we determine how the job is done, to what standards, and how those standards are then measured. We introduce the plan, and work with each level of the company on implementing change.

New Beginning

Once all new processes and standards are in place, we work to make sure they are tracked, measured, and reviewed for accountability. We continue with the standardization process over and over again, raising the bar from one level to the next. There is no room for complacency here. By this time, the organization has married its culture and language to new and improved operations, propelling it forward toward continued growth and success. It's a fascinating process. The more we refine, optimize, and integrate all the pieces, the more negativity the organization and people within it shed, and the healthier it all becomes. It's like cleaning up a masterpiece painting that has aged over the years. Underneath the dirt and grime lies a beautiful picture that needed to be painstakingly cleaned and rediscovered. Sometimes we act as the artist to create the painting from a blank canvas, but more often than not, the image exists, and we uncover and enhance what is already there.

Of course, not all new beginnings smoothly boost a business to success textbook-style. People are people, and they are perfectly imperfect. In business, it's about survival, so most people are quite wary of change and how it will affect them personally. One manager at a company I worked with threw a stapler at me. I found out through one of our routine interviews about some not-so-palatable things he had done personally, that went on to affect him professionally. All those kinds of details come out eventually, because we have to ferret out all of the dysfunction to create a strong and healthy framework moving forward.

> Playing the part is acceptable, hence the phrase "Fake it 'til you make it", but you still need to be you in playing the part.

Restructuring can also get messy whenever a shift in power takes place; like when a company is bought out, but the owner stays on to work. It can be tricky to pass that power over to another leader with a different system and culture in place. Usually the new owners place the former owner in a position where his or her talents are best-suited. Similarly, even when there is a clear succession plan and well-defined transfer of power between old and new, the entire company must be indoctrinated into this change.

The renowned writer, politician, and philosopher Niccolo Machiavelli wrote about transfer of power and change in his book *The Prince* way back in 1513. It's interesting how much of what he wrote still applies today:

"Reforming an existing order is one of the most dangerous and difficult things a prince can do. People are naturally resistant to change and reform. Those who benefited from the old order resist fiercely. Those who can benefit from the new order will resist less fiercely – but the new order is unfamiliar, and they are not certain it will live up to its promises".

The Prince is all about how to transcend your passion and duplicate yourself, growing your kingdom. Machiavelli extensively discussed ruling and conquering in notoriously controversial ways relating to politics back then, but some of what he did and said made sense. For instance, he spoke very differently to various groups of people within his kingdom. He spoke to taxpayers differently than how he spoke to the peasants, or how he spoke to his staff. He had a different language for each of these groups to make them respect and love him. If he had spoken to his staff the same way he had spoken to the peasants—all loving and caring and monotonous—his staff would probably have gotten away with a lot! It's human nature to take what you can get. In each voice, though, he remained within his authentic self. He was a manager to his staff, a caretaker for the peasants, and a servant of the taxpayers. It's important to be genuine, honest, sincere, and then admit when you can't be. Playing the part is acceptable, hence the phrase "Fake it 'til you make it", but you still need to be you in playing the part.

Machiavelli was also a huge advocate of continuous learning and improvement, which is what marrying language and culture with operations strives to do. Continuous learning means capturing experiences and truly leaning in to be optimally engaged. It means reflecting on what could have been done differently, then understanding that and applying it going forward. Continuous improvement is result of the application of continuous learning. It means paying it forward and setting an example, sharing expertise, and teaching those who are authentic and paying attention. Great leaders grasp all of this and build loyalty through continuous learning and improvement layered throughout an organization. These principles build momentum in cultivating excellence, and are what iBG models are all about.

"The Playbook"

Once an organization has gone through the process of change, whether that be in branding or in operations, that organization is then issued its own customized playbook to follow. This playbook, just as with its sports counterpart, contains information (plays) that all people within the organization follow. It maps out exactly how each person should do his or her job, and to what standard, in order for them to be collectively successful as a team. It lists contingency options for when things don't go as planned. It also allows for improvements to the system as needed, within the parameters of the models. When each person follows the playbook, all are in sync, and the team is poised to win.

Language Progression Image - The Journey to Fluency

Integrated Branding & Operations Process

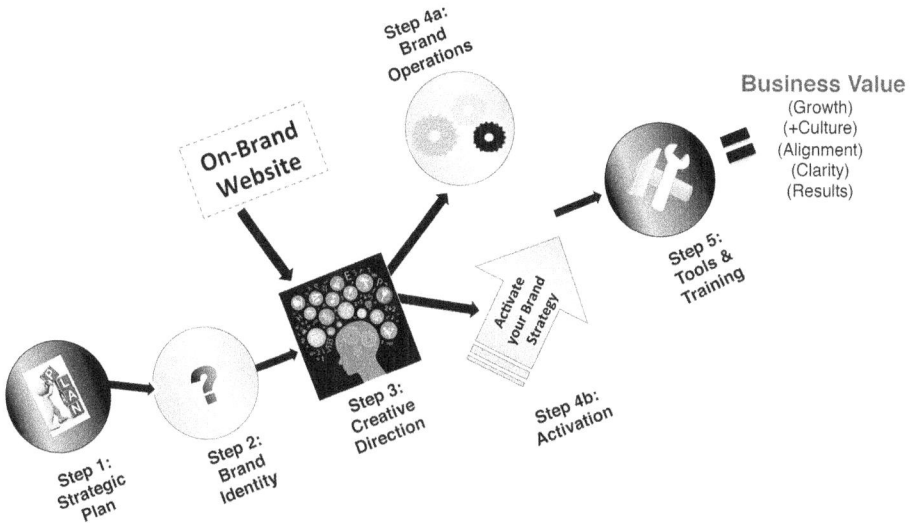

HOW DOES YOUR GARDEN GROW?

*"If your actions inspire others
to dream more, learn more, do more,
and become more, you are a leader."*

John Quincy Adams

If leading were easy, everyone would want to be the manager—or even better—the president of the company. It seems that our innate human nature causes us to criticize how others do things, and insists that we know better. Look at all the armchair quarterbacks out there watching football every Sunday afternoon, shouting, *"The referee must be blind!"* or *"How could the quarterback miss that throw?!"* or *"The receiver is a butterfingers!"*

How does a leader become excellent, earning loyalty and respect from those he or she manages? Which characteristics determine the best leaders? Who motivates the people at the top, and holds them accountable? Contrary to what you might think, it's a two-way street. The top and the bottom of an organization work together to motivate and support one another, fortifying the business as a whole.

We've extensively discussed the models for both Identity and Operations, and all of the many processes that fall within their scopes. It takes an immense amount of time and effort to introduce these models, and achieve mastery throughout a company across all levels of employees. Truly successful implementation will result in leaders being held accountable by their own employees for following the models, and continuing to strive toward higher standards. This happens every now and then at iBG. We have a system for scheduling, including a master calendar that all our employees can access. One of us might be onsite at a client's business, and pull up the master calendar online. Thinking he or she is being helpful by scheduling the client's next meeting, that person places a new appointment on the calendar. On the other end, our master scheduler will have scheduled another appointment on the calendar at the same time, and now he or she is double booked. That employee is not enhancing the model, but instead is messing with it! Therefore, it is our best practice to have one person managing the calendar, and scheduling appointments. The model shows that our employees call, email, or text the office, and one designated person will schedule the client. We hold each other accountable to that! At the same time, when our inside office staff members have tasks to complete, we are clear and concise about what we need from one another, and when we need it. If there are questions, we talk, and clarify it immediately. We have great systems in place for that, and we stick to them.

Here's another example from the past, showing accountability measures in place: A giant board of Post-It Notes with staff goals written on them hung on the wall in my office. Anytime a goal was completed, staff would come into my office, and initial their individual notes. The next time we met as a group, those goals were all right there for us to review and celebrate; or to discuss any hurdles hindering them from being completed. Today, it might be as simple as a mid-day phone call asking for status on a task. If the job hasn't been completed, employees will always give me an estimated completion time and date, and reasons for delay. That's accountability in action!

The goal of a leader should be to mentor, and develop other people to manage and "grow the garden". If you never nourish the people at the bottom, they will never nourish the leader in turn, and no one will blossom. In fact, a well-lead employee actively looking to grow and promote upward in an organization will make his or her leader blossom and look good. That employee is the stem growing from a strong, rooted foundation. That stem supports the blossom at the top, and the top continues to cultivate the bottom. It's reciprocal.

Employees must be cultivated from the bottom up through a solid foundation of modeling, education, encouragement, and accountability standards among other things. A leader should mentor (LIVE) the culture, and speak the language, so that employees confidently follow. It's not enough to know it; actions speak louder than words. When we implement a new corporate culture and language, or new operations and accountability processes, we simultaneously implement these models with an approach we call "Top-Down Bottom-Up"; all levels of an organization learning and implementing their roles in change at the same time.

The models are designed to truly solve a problem, and produce a solid answer, not simply slap a Band-Aid on it.

Leaders are trained to teach, model, and filter information down throughout the rest of the company. Change can be hard, and it can also be scary. Leaders confidently show that this new path is not only safe, but the best path toward individual success, and the collective success of the company. At the same time, employees are indoctrinated, and included in these processes from the beginning. They are given a chance to ask questions, give feedback, and be part of change as it's happening. This ensures that all employees feel they have been heard. They are important, and they matter as part of building their culture. They take pride in it! Through this Top-Down Bottom-Up approach, the shift travels through all ranks of the company at the same time for the most efficient and thorough integration. The top cultivates the bottom, and the bottom nourishes the top.

Change is always well-thought out and planned in advance, taking into consideration potential risks and outcomes. It is enacted with clear goals in mind, and envisions long-term results. It should never be impulsively imposed in reaction to a short-term or one-time problem, as in corrective strategy. A highly reactive leader will create fear and distrust amongst employees, and rarely discovers the root cause of a problem. A proactive leader thinks before he or she acts, and follows the model using perfective strategy. The models are designed to truly solve a problem, and produce a solid answer, not simply slap a Band-Aid on it.

Good leaders want to share knowledge with their employees, equipping them to better make decisions on a day-to-day basis. Add in some encouragement, along with permission to make a mistake every now and then, and you will nurture and grow employees with the tools to thrive. It goes back to the assumption that we are not perfect beings, and we will make mistakes. Too much rigidity creates a culture full of fear of failure, and stifles initiative and creativity. Mistakes are perfect learning opportunities when handled in the correct way.

Sure, certain personality types may seem better suited to leadership roles. They almost always portray a sense of confidence and certainty, but you can be sure that they don't always have all the answers, or necessarily know in each moment exactly what action to take. Strong leaders know how to punt as needed, but also possess the knowledge and experience to know when and how to do that within the parameters of the models and the culture. They know and continue to learn how best to exemplify, teach, motivate, and uphold standards. Most importantly, they embody passion for what they do, and eagerly transfer that passion on to others in order to perpetuate success.

HORSES

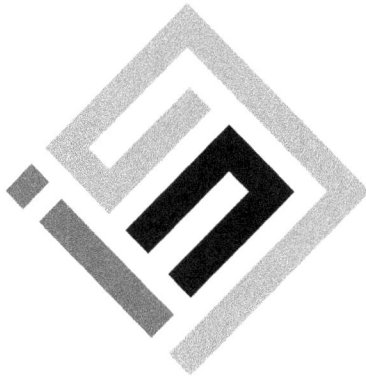

"Horses teach you patience,
and how to do things the right way
so you can get the right result."

Lyle Lovett

I'm still not entirely sure why I felt compelled to approach the unfamiliar barn on that day. It had been a tough time in my life and in business, and on that one particularly awful day, I drove, like I had every day, past the horses standing next to the old, weathered, white barn. They never seemed to move, but just stood there motionless day after day, and I had to find out why. I broke routine and abruptly turned into the driveway. I walked up to the house next to the barn, knocked on the door, and asked the lady who answered, "What's the story with the horses?" She replied that they were giving them a home temporarily until they were adopted and placed elsewhere. Before I knew it, I was the new guardian of "Bella", a diva mare with attitude. I leased her from her foster parents, so she could stay put, and I could conveniently drop by the barn on the way home from work.

I didn't set out to adopt a horse that afternoon, but something drew me to Bella in that moment. I know that I was tired, searching for something, and felt led there as naturally as if it had been a scheduled part of my day. I now know that it was absolutely meant to be part of my journey. Granted, I went through a horse phase as a young boy growing up. I read *Black Beauty* and *The Black Stallion* and asked my parents for a horse; and like most parents, they said no. I'm sure they knew the vast amount of time and resources a horse would require, and as restaurant owners, other priorities took precedent over indulging in their youngest son's horse fantasies. So here I was, all grown up and able to make the responsible decision to commit my own time and resources to this sweet, yet stubborn, beautifully wild horse.

I had danced this dance before, just in a different setting. Bella wouldn't even let me in her stall in the beginning; most clients aren't very open with me on the first day either, so I imagined I could do this! In retrospect, it's probably good that I was naïve. I didn't know what I didn't know, so Bella and I figured it out together. Each time I tried to enter her stall, she would rear up, then proceed to hiss, snort, buck, and kick. She was not having any part of me in her space. I tested my boundaries by first opening the door to the stall, then standing there waiting, and slowly strolling in. It's not like I just threw open the door and charged her, but those attempts were still miserable, and we weren't getting anywhere. I realized this was going to take a while, so I decided to read to her. I chose two of the longest books I knew and loved: *To Kill a Mockingbird* and *Gone with the Wind*. They would give me plenty to do while an ornery Miss Bella tolerated my presence. I only hoped to make a breakthrough, and that our relationship would prove not to be as tumultuous as Scarlett and Rhett's!

I began by reading just outside her door. Gradually, I moved into the doorway and waited for her to react. Week after week I challenged her, sometimes moving forward with ease, and then just as quickly losing ground again. Eventually, I found myself sitting on a stool inside her stall, and realized that I was working with her…working with myself. This was an exercise in patience, trust, and relationship building. It couldn't be forced, but had to evolve in its own time. We were both immersed in the experience, and navigating how to do this. After about two weeks of sitting on my stool inside her stall and dancing this dance—I knew her moves and she knew mine—she pinned me up against the wall with her butt, and I had a crucial decision to make: I could panic (not the wisest choice with a 1,200-lb. insecure animal in an enclosed space), or I could go with it. I chose the latter. I took my book, placed it square upon her butt, got comfortable, and continued reading. This was our routine. Then, one day while I was using her butt as my table yet again, she quickly took a step forward with her front right foot, pivoted with her front left foot counterclockwise, and put her head right in my book as if to say, "What's so exciting in there that you'll just go ahead and ignore my rude gestures?!" I was finally face to face with this majestic animal, and it was my move. I touched her face, petted her blaze, and moved the book all around her head. She tolerated that pretty well, so now I'm thinking I can ride her! Again, here was optimism and naïveté at its finest.

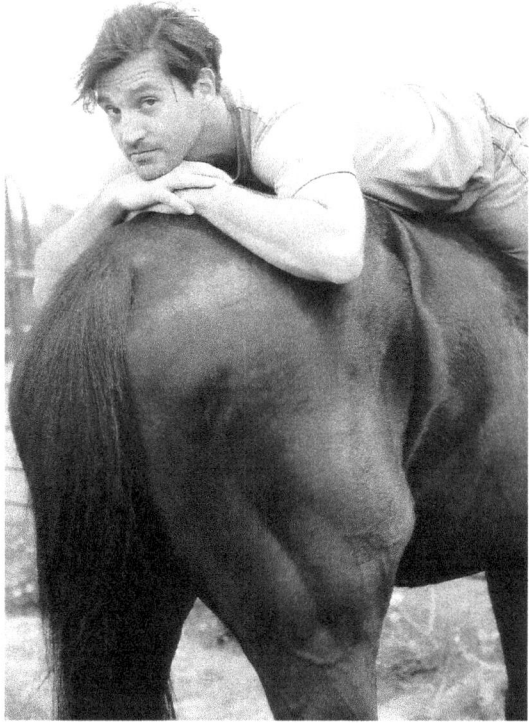

Progressing to the point of actually sitting on Bella's back and riding her took an excruciatingly long time, but each and every second it took to get there was valuable time spent. I was doing all of this work with Bella without any expertise or knowledge, so we figured out our own way of training. Throughout that very raw, made-up process, we found meaning in each and every step. We could have followed a very tried and true training program, and we might have benefited greatly from that. But then I wouldn't have been able to learn, experience, and engage in our journey the way I did. At the time, I stepped up to the experience, and immersed myself in it without worrying if I was doing it wrong. Through this, Bella and I now have a bond that is uniquely our own. Of course, I did eventually ride her. I didn't put a bridle on her, or a bit in her mouth right away, because I didn't know how. I simply fit a halter on her head with two lead ropes attached, and just like that I was riding a horse. I'd watch others ride and learn from them, then I'd adjust until it felt right. I began by riding bareback because again, I didn't own a saddle much less know what to do with one. The sensations that I garnered from riding bareback, and feeling the power of sitting atop a nearly one-ton animal was like an out-of-body experience. It's not like riding a bike because you have no control, you have only trust. I wasn't aware of any of the situations I should have been fearful of, so when I fell off, I automatically got back up on her. I didn't feel any sense of doubt, worry, or fear.

I'll never forget the very first time I fell off Bella. We were booking it, cruising down a narrow lane, and a deer suddenly leapt out directly in front of us. We couldn't escape anywhere, because we had entered a thick section of woods that prevented her from going forward. I woke up on the ground to her nudging my body. If you spent enough time with Bella, you'd know she is a total prima donna. She's not affectionate. She's not attention seeking, but rather plays hard to get. Somehow, we had built this camaraderie and partnership. Together, we trusted one another with fearlessness and fierceness. It was a turning point.

After that, time marched on and soon it was winter. Every day I drove to the barn from Milwaukee, where I was living at the time, and I had developed the habit of packing a bag on Thursday night, grabbing my beloved yellow lab Sofi, and crashing at the barn for the weekend. It was cold and snowing heavily outside, but inside the barn it was warm and dry. The sweet smell of horses and hay made it a welcome sanctuary from the harsh winter. By this time, I had adopted two other horses, Champ and Snickers, so they were now part of our little equine family. I groomed everyone, made some hot apple cider, and relaxed by a fire near the barn. Meanwhile, my friends were furiously sending texts back and forth to determine when and where we were going to meet up that night. We usually met at a bar not far from the barn, so it was convenient for me to join them. I let them know I would meet them later, and that I was at the barn. They had no idea that I led this secret life. This was a huge shift. I remember feeling guilty that I had missed all that quality time at the barn because I had been spending time at the bar with my friends instead. It was a transformational moment in how I was starting to live.

> When you're fluent with a horse, your body is completely automatic and reactive in sync with the animal in the moment. When you're fluent in your business language and culture, you react to any situation appropriately and in the moment too.

These horses have influenced me to the point that if I don't get my horse time I notice, and other people notice. It's positively shaped my life in terms of my health, energy, emotions, and responsibilities. They gave me purpose. Bella, Champ, and Snickers needed me, and perhaps I needed them even more. They made me feel alive, empowered, fueled, and energized. Nothing felt hard or difficult to do after time spent with them. On the other hand, when I was flying high, they humbled me and brought me down to earth. Beyond that, they gave me perspective and made me mindful. Accidents happen when you're not in the moment with a horse, so when it's raining, I'm more conscious of riding on level ground so we don't slip. I think about the width of the lanes we ride on, so they have enough room to turn. I personally simmer down and become more balanced around them because they will pick up on my nervous energy and freak out if I don't. Really though, that whole training process was no different from speaking a new language or stepping into a different culture. Each barn has its own culture. Each stall within each barn is different, just as each department or office can be different within a company. It's amazing.

Consequently, I'm not afraid to dive into a new culture. I don't fear pitching to anyone. I figure if I can interpret these horses, I can interpret any person in any situation. Horses communicate primarily in a non-verbal way. They do make noises to read or misread, but you have to be very in-tune and intuitive about it. If you're not paying attention, you'll miss a sign like ears flat back against a head, or a very twitchy tail. Some people would say, "I don't know what happened! That horse just wigged out all of a sudden!"

I say *you missed it*. You weren't paying attention and weren't completely in the moment in mind and in body. There are cues that look obvious when you look back at them, and place them into context at that point in time. It's the perfect summary of marrying language with culture to come to a place of mutual understanding and respect. You don't think about what your body is telling you to do when you react to a horse. When you're fluent with a horse, it's completely automatic and reactive in sync with the animal in the moment. When you're fluent in your business language and culture, you react to any situation appropriately and in the moment too. To me, working with horses creates the perfect metaphor for both work and life.

Sofi
My best
companion

Champ & Bella
My teachers

Snickers
My student

Relaxing with Bella is just as exhilarating as riding. We love being together and sharing quality time with one another.

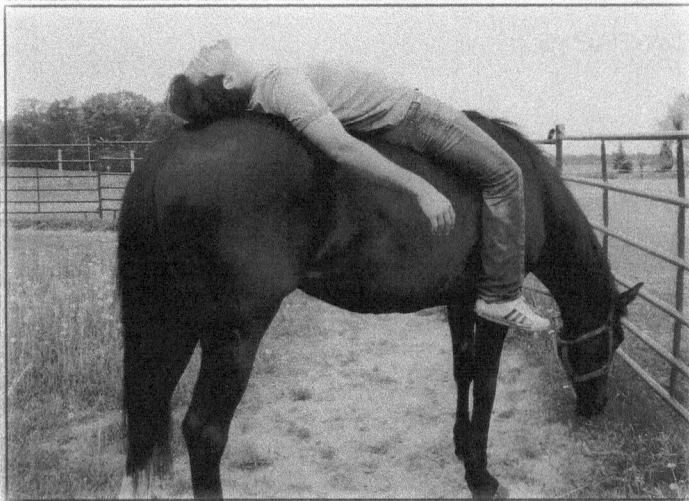

A place of peace, safety, & trust. A time of calmness, energy, & giving back to one another.

Play

Energize

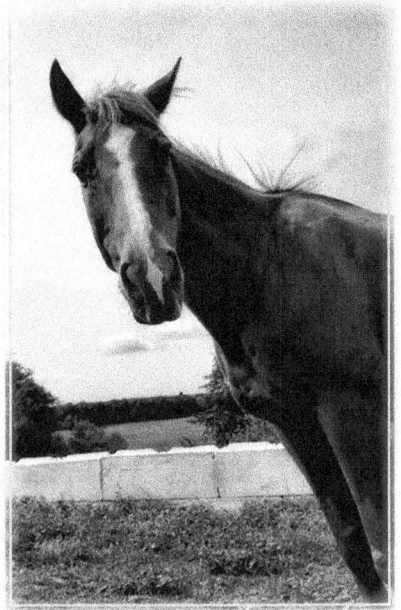

Relax

Eat

Talk

Love

Rest is needed
before horsing
around, but Sofi
always wonders,
"When are we going
back to the farm?"

Although Champ can move, his preferred pace is slow. We know each other's movements and when I'm on him, I am able to truly enjoy my surroundings. Being in nature with Champ is a completely different experience to enjoy.

Integrating,
collaborating, &
partnering.

They fuel & motivate me.

On the trail

UNDERSTANDING

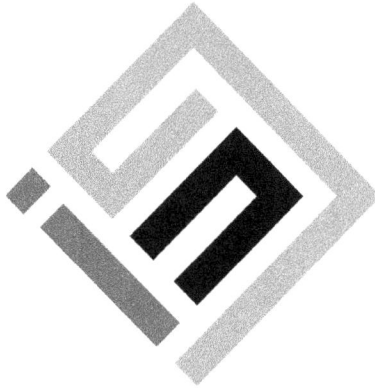

"Competing at the highest level is not about winning. It's about preparation, courage, understanding and nurturing your people, and heart. Winning is the result."

Joe Torre

We've talked about the models. We've discussed the processes. We've taken a journey through learning language and building a culture. We agree that it takes more than just raw knowledge or talent to lead, and to succeed. We need balance in our lives, and outside experiences teach us wisdom beyond the business; leading us toward the best versions of ourselves. But in the end, does all this stuff really work? Let's take a closer look.

Case Study #1
An Entrepreneur and a Boutique

The fashion and retail world is fast-moving and ever-changing. It's difficult enough to stay one step ahead of current trends, much less match those trends to what local consumers want and need. One smart executive was up for the challenge. This budding entrepreneur always dreamed of opening an exclusive boutique. Finally, with years of business experience behind her, the time was right to live that dream. Having completed a market and competitor analysis, it became clear that a high-end boutique was just what the local audience needed. This new boutique would differentiate itself from competitors by focusing on a high-quality fashion experience, including attention to detail and the needs of the customer, in a calm, exclusive environment. From the moment a guest walked through the door, she would be warmly welcomed by a highly-trained, friendly fashion consultant. Through building a relationship and learning her story, the boutique's consultants uncover each guest's unique style to best outfit her with clothes she will wear and love!

The owner's extensive business experience led her to zero in on building standard policies and operational procedures for this new business from the very beginning, and iBG collaborated with the owner and her staff to design and implement these processes. We also provided creative and operational guidance as the business launched, and throughout the first year of operation. During the operational design phase, it became evident that the brand strategy and marketing approach needed to be upgraded. We worked on brand clarity, improving the website, creating and writing policies to guide several departments, defining employee roles and responsibilities, and implementing an employee performance evaluation.

Throughout this entire process, the owner also better defined her specific leadership role. She led by example, being held accountable for her role, as well as holding others accountable for theirs. Most importantly, *she led by internally motivating her staff toward their highest potential, and then holding them accountable to that*. This was not a dictatorial culture guided by rules and consequences. Employees fully owned their roles and responsibilities, because they had helped develop them from the very beginning. They strived to do well because they *wanted* to do well; and they wanted to do well largely because this particular owner wholly embodied her business's identity, language, and style in LIVING her brand!

As the owner's areas of expertise grew into the retail industry specifically, her responsibilities, and the roles of her managers were slightly redefined. Since then, this boutique has been wildly successful, surpassing all initial six-month and one-year milestones for sales and profit. This retail business exemplifies how entrepreneurs must plan all aspects of their business prior to opening. It took in-depth work from the beginning to truly understand the boutique's identity and brand, operational processes, and staff roles and accountabilities. Putting all these pieces together earned the owner, and her dedicated staff, the fast track to success!

Case Study #2
A Media Company Flourishes

Some businesses have enormous potential to grow, but growth doesn't magically occur simply because you wish it to be; you need a plan in place to make it happen! The high-level leaders of this company adamantly pushed for growth, as they clearly saw potential and opportunity; but the company wasn't yet structured or poised to reach that potential. It became evident early on that their sales model at the time drastically needed to change. It featured multiple sales teams each selling only one of the many advertising media options offered. The sales team was also too large, resulting in low revenue per sales person, and little chance for individual growth. Worse yet, customers resented having to meet with several different sales representatives from the same company to purchase all the avenues needed to create a successful advertising campaign. iBG recommended that this business flip that sales model upside-down. It needed to move from selling only one product per sales representative across a large sales team, to a smaller team offering a portfolio of various media products per sales representative. Simply, they needed to grow revenue, while reducing costs, to improve the company's profitability. This shift in sales structure created a much more efficient, and effective way for their clients to choose from a variety of media solutions. They could work with one sales representative to customize a package specific to their business' marketing needs. Simultaneously, sales staff numbers were reduced, allowing each representative to become much stronger individually. Educating leadership and staff on what exactly a brand means, and how the company's brand could grow into a portfolio of products, resulted in a much more efficient structure. Following this shift, the focus moved toward integrating the company's business plan for growth and increased profits together with their new brand and identity strategy. iBG once again worked the "Top-Down Bottom-Up" approach with all teams simultaneously. Employees from the bottom of the hierarchy to the top and back again learned together, supporting one another through change. It swept across all departments including production, programming, sales, marketing, and administration.

In the end, not only did sales staff numbers dramatically reduce from a total of sixty to eighteen, but the company significantly gained market share. It also increased the amount of money invested per client, and created a broader reach to customers within the market. An epic success story, this company doubled its revenue over five years as an iBG client. Living the brand from the inside-out, educating individual sales team members on the wider variety of media platforms, and then pulling them together as a team to add more value to customers, led to this company reaching its highest aspirations!

Case Study #3
Hospitality Company Plans Transition

What happens when three friends, who are also co-owners of a very successful company, begin transitioning into the next phases of their lives beyond the business world? With some serious strategic planning, perhaps they can each live a life of leisure after all the hard work is done! These three executives combined their distinctly different personalities with a deep-rooted friendship that allowed them to build a thriving, growing business. They balanced each other very well in both personalities, and skill sets. They were so integrated into the daily operations of the business though, that the future of it continuing beyond them hadn't been discussed in enough detail. These men had built a strong culture that was unified enough to keep business moving forward, but too many questions remained:

◈ Where are we going as individuals?

◈ Where are we going as a company?

◈ Are we working as smart as we could be?

◈ Are we able to continue working at this capacity, and at this age for much longer?

◈ How are we going to transition when we reach the point of diminishing our time working the business, and entering retirement?

The three owners decided that iBG's Strategic Planning Program would best help them resolve these questions, and propel them successfully forward. They began with the first of three phases, the "Target Exercise". The Target Exercise is effective in that it forces you to dig deep. It's best facilitated by someone objective, and separate from the organization, people, or team. It requires perseverance to see a difficult question all the way through to the true answer. It's much easier, and more comfortable in the short-term, to avoid and procrastinate. In this case, The Target Exercise brought several previously unasked questions to the forefront for the team to analyze. Together, we compared and examined these questions, discovering that some were the same amongst the owners, and some were different. We took each question, asked it, dissected it down into deeper detail, and asked it over and over again until we received the same answer every time. Sometimes it takes extensive probing, and whittling down before getting to the heart of the matter, and finally reaching the best conclusion. For example, a Target Exercise dialogue might look like this:

Problem: You have a D in math.
Goal: You want to raise your grade to an A
Q: How are you going to raise your grade?
A: I'm going to work harder

This is where many people get stuck. "How" is a complicated question, and one that is easy to avoid for now. But without finding an answer and creating a plan, raising the grade to an A won't happen intentionally. It may only happen by accident, or luck!

Q: How are you going to work harder?
A: I'm going to study longer at night.

Q: How exactly are you going to study?

A: I'm going to go online and do practice problems.

Q: What if you don't understand a concept?

A: I'm going to email my teacher, and meet with him outside of class. I will also make a note when I don't understand a concept as it's introduced in class, so I can ask the question right away.

Now we're getting somewhere! You can see how more detailed questions were revealed as we continued to probe towards a true answer to the problem at hand. Now let's look at a legitimate question in the workplace:

Q: "How long do you want to work?"

A: I want to work for five years

Q: How are you going to do that?

The answer is actually quite complicated. Back at our hospitality business, this process ultimately sparked a series of complex, diverse, and long-overdue conversations for the three partners. It set the stage for relaxed discussion, during time set aside in the middle of the work day, to focus on the future, and life outside of work. The approach was relaxed and accommodating, giving the owners the opportunity to focus on issues they had put off for too long, or sometimes hadn't even considered yet. Ultimately, iBG helped gather all these thoughts and realizations, and put them together into an organized action plan. That plan was implemented, and a system put in place to track each step, ensuring continued growth and success now, and well into the future.

Success is not a given in business. It requires hard work, planning, and a willingness to get uncomfortable in the process. Each of the business owners highlighted here were able to break out of routine thought patterns, old outdated work processes, and address seemingly unanswerable questions in order to take themselves and their businesses to the next level. Through following their Playbooks and the models, they were able to confidently lead their employees to also achieve individual successes contributing toward the greater good of the company. They built up employee confidence to buy into change, and instilled the belief that they, as employees, could make a positive difference in the world both in business and in life.

SUGAR, PART II

"The keys to brand success are self-definition, transparency, authenticity and accountability."

Simon Mainwaring

Sugar
(Part 2)

FADE IN:

EXT. LUXURY HOTEL EXTERIOR FULL VIEW

DISSOLVE TO:

INT. BOARD ROOM

THE EXECUTIVE TEAM of a high-end hospitality company sits at one end of a huge board table in the middle of the room. They wait attentively in anticipation of a lower-level manager meeting soon to take place. The purpose of the meeting was to integrate the next level of management into the new corporate brand culture, and operating procedures.

                    CUT TO:

INT. HALLWAY OUTSIDE THE BOARD ROOM

Outside the board room, THE MANAGERS
anxiously fidget outside the entrance to the
room, waiting for the doors to open, and
the meeting to start.

                    CUT BACK TO:

INT. BOARD ROOM

MICHAEL, the meeting facilitator, gazes
around inside the room, his eyes finally
coming to rest on the coffee condiments
sitting on the table: cream and sugar. He
walks over to the table, picks up a handful
of sugar packets, and slowly walks back in
front of the executive team at the front of
the room.

            MICHAEL (to the executive team)
      "We've already gone over the agenda for
    the meeting, but I have one more item. I'm
      going to do something to the management
    team when they walk in, but I don't want
           any of you to comment on it.
                Just roll with it."

Michael walks over to the doors to let the
managers into the room, but before opening
them, he tears open the sugar packets, and
dumps them onto the floor just inside the
entrance way to the room. He glances over
at the executive board, and placing his
index finger in front of his mouth, gives
them the "Shhhhh" sign.

CUT TO:

OUTSIDE THE BOARD ROOM, the doors open, and the executive team comes into view. Their faces are expressionless. The managers walk into the board room, fill in the empty seats at the board table, and sit down.

MICHAEL addresses the room
"Hi, my name is Michael. It's nice to meet you, and I'll be able to go around the room and hear who you are and what you do on a one-on-one basis in just a minute, but first I have a question. Who in this room lives the brand of this company? Raise your hand."

CAMERA PANS THE ROOM:

Slowly, one by one, every hand in the room goes up.

MICHAEL
"Great! It seems like you are all very engaged and active. You love coming to work! Then why would you walk across an entryway, of all places, and not pick up the sugar packets that were on the ground? I'd like everybody who lives the brand of this hospitality company to please raise your hand."

CAMERA PANS THE ROOM:

Only the executive team raises their hands.

FADE TO BLACK…

What happened here? The executive team was most certainly shocked that not one of their many managers paused to pick up the mess in the doorway. NOT ONE. They all saw it, because they stepped around it and over it, but each person deliberately moved on forward into the room and sat down without hesitation. We could surmise that the context of the meeting distracted them; wondering what it was about and how long it would take. A group mentality might have overtaken the managers, so that after the first one or two people ignored the mess, the rest of them followed suit. I didn't coach the executive team to raise their hands, and the rest of the room to sit motionless when I asked who lived the brand the second time. I can only imagine that the executive team would have, in fact, picked up the sugar packets had they been the group walking into the room that day. We at iBG had spent the past six weeks working with them, and leading them to develop their brand culture, operations, and accountability, so they were primed to apply what they had learned. This scenario clearly illustrated for them where the rest of the company stood in terms of truly LIVING the brand. They weren't LIVING the high standards by which this luxury hospitality company proudly advertised itself to the world. Had they embodied those, they would have picked up the mess without hesitation. We had to get them to the point that they were immersed in their culture, and speaking their language at work ALL the time. They had to learn to overcome distraction, excitement, lethargy, indifference, and any other gamut of situations and emotions they might encounter throughout a typical day. It turned out that the main reason no one acted autonomously in picking up the sugar packets, or raising their hands, was fear. We uncovered that explanation through our exercises and hard work in the months following that day. We figured out the barriers to these employees being able to act innately, without thinking, to the standards that this company expected. It took a strong team effort to work through the models, and get them to that point, but we did it together. Like directing an orchestra, there is nothing more satisfying than when all the instruments come together to play a symphony in perfect rhythm, and harmony. Each person plays his or her part with precision, and passion. That is the result of a long process of practice for understanding, and then putting all the pieces together—leading to total integration.

LETTING GO

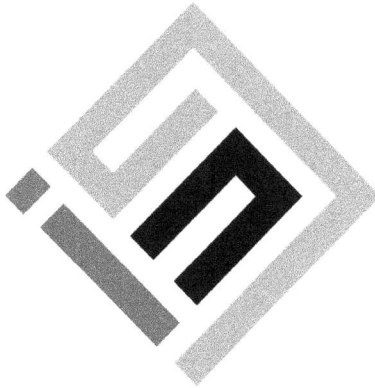

*"Some of us think holding on makes us strong;
but sometimes it is letting go."*

Hermann Hesse

In business, as in life, some things will never grow no matter how much you try to nurture and cultivate them. Not everything grows at the same pace, and growth sometimes occurs only in a certain season or period of time, regardless of the amount of effort put forth. It doesn't matter how much I yearn to see something thrive, evolve, reach new heights, and bloom. I can't magically will it to be a certain way. So, there comes a time to release at least partial control of a situation, give it some space, and let it be. For me, that's much easier said than done. I can know it's time to back off on an intellectual level, but emotionally that can be very difficult; especially when I see unreached potential. It doesn't matter if that is regarding a person, horse, or business situation. In the past, I have chosen to give all of myself and still watch it fall short of expectations. Unfortunately, this is part of the human condition, and the sooner we all come to terms with that, I think the healthier we'll be! The added bonus is that often, these situations can be optimized anyway *because* we back off. Giving 100% is no guaranteed formula for success.

I recently parted ways with a client I'd worked with intensively over the past couple of years. Our relationship had been difficult for a number of reasons, and although I've ruminated about it and analyzed the circumstances, in the end none of that matters. Each of us had the ability to continue to persevere despite our differences, but we mutually decided we had come as far forward together as we were willing to travel, and it was time to let go. They were a complicated group of people, needing me to help them create structure and organization that directly conflicted with the very loose and creative culture they thrived upon. At one point, they did consider being able to capture what their culture was all about, blend it with operational structure, and grow business. They understood the Identity Model at multiple levels. They are a very intelligent business with very intelligent employees, but the Operations Models and all they entail completely baffled them. Standard operating procedures, job descriptions, and evaluations all clashed directly with their creative processes and non-conforming culture. Although they were capable of being strategic, they strongly resisted anything too formal, for fear of jeopardizing their creative image. I understood that from a marketing standpoint, but couldn't personally support their resistance to structure because of their dire need for some operational parameters, and a well thought out succession plan. So, to move them forward, I had to let go of my recommendation to focus on the operations side, and instead guide them through the Identity Model, focusing on language and culture.

They embraced the process fully. It wasn't easy by any means. They struggled to tell their stories, and when I collected their relevant examples and transcribed them verbatim, they didn't like them. At that point I completely let go, gave them the process to own with some instruction, and they immersed. They immersed, and they succeeded in completing it! They were able to move forward because they did it on their own. My intervention and my standards would have been barriers to them. Releasing control was not only paramount to their success, it was liberating for me. In the end, I was proud of the progress they made. Although they didn't ultimately meet the operational goals I initially envisioned for them, they advanced to a place beyond where we began, and are poised to meet those goals when ready, sometime in the future.

This past year has been a year of change for me, both

personally and professionally. When you live your brand in both business and life, you are authentic. Your values transcend barriers, and you can meet struggle or conflict with all the tools you need to work through it and move forward. I find that I'm able to apply lessons learned in business to my personal life, and lessons learned in my personal life to business. I shouldn't compromise my values within either realm. To clarify, when I'm at work, my mind and intentions are at work, and when I'm not at work, I'm with my horses. As has been established, they ground me, keep me humble, constantly learning, and challenged.

I have had to learn to let go of various circumstances with each one of my horses recently, for a variety of reasons. Sometimes we choose to let go, and sometimes we are forced. I struggle with forced letting go the most. I have a confession to make; Snickers has been "my" horse for the past few years, without my officially having guardianship of him. He came along with the barn where my other two adopted horses, Bella and Champ lived. The barn owner was unable to take care of Snickers, so that fell to me over the course of twelve years. He is a cute, feisty, speckled gelding that went with my "herd". I was the only one who rode him and became his main caretaker. When circumstances dictated that I move Bella and Champ recently, I always assumed that Snickers would come along. Unfortunately, when push came to shove and moving day loomed, Snickers' official owners chose to offer him up at a price well above market value. I could follow my heart, or follow logic, and after being taken advantage of throughout the years, had to choose logic. I continue to struggle with this decision today, now that Bella and Champ are moved to a new barn, and Snickers is gone. I don't know where he is, and that sits heavy on my heart. I hope that he is well taken care of and has found a new home. Unfortunately, as any other animal lovers reading this no doubt realize, I can't adopt them all. I can only live best within my capabilities, and I have to let the rest go.

Bella is another story altogether. As I described earlier,

she is a one-man horse and my pride and joy. Throughout our training together, she has let go and stripped off anything that past owners have dressed her with or imposed upon her. She and I have an understanding. Part of that understanding is that she insists on living life with as much energy as I will allow. She is a difficult horse to contain. She takes such good care of me when I'm riding her, that I feel as comfortable on her back as I do when relaxing on my couch at home–minus moving forty miles per hour and jumping creeks! I feel a safety and security when riding her that is indescribable. To get to this point meant letting go of trying to control her stubborn personality, her anxious behavior, her antsy footing, her head position. She might not be conventional, but to force her to conform to others' standards would mean taking away her essence. She might not be perfectly behaved, but we could not be more one if she and I were a centaur. She knows two speeds: gallop or backing up a little bit, but I love it and so does she! I'm thankful that she has taught me not to embrace perfection, but rather to meet a person (or horse) where he or she is. That is a lesson I use every day, whether embracing family, friends, business associates, equine or canine. I know Bella's wisdom will continue to serve me well no matter where life or business takes me.

Champ is not nearly as complex as Bella, but the lesson he recently taught me about more literally letting go is priceless. I recently moved both Champ and Bella to a different farm. I should have made the move a long time ago, but I was concerned about leaving the remaining two horses I didn't own at the old barn and breaking up the herd. It was difficult, but once we finally made the move, I realized that my horses were fine. We aren't far from their old home, but when we ride they don't make any moves to glance toward their old pasture, much less make a break to head back.

The only challenge has been that when I ride one, the other is left alone at the barn without the companionship of the other horse. Both horses acted up when I attempted to ride one or the other, to the point that I was afraid they would hurt themselves. I had to come up with a solution that wouldn't necessarily involve adopting another horse and taking on another project, so I resorted to riding one horse while leading the other on a lead line. It wasn't ideal, especially in the cold winter months when I could barely feel my hands yet needed to be capable of directing two horses at once. They adjusted smoothly; behaving well as we moved through our gaits, completed courses and drills, and although not completely safe, moved into an all-out gallop every now and then. Little by little, as the weather grew warmer along with our confidence, I began to entertain the idea of dropping the lead line and allowing the second horse to follow freely. Other "horse people" might call me crazy, but I know my horses and their capabilities. I began to set the lead line down in front of me on the saddle while keeping an eye on the horse I was leading. I did this multiple times over the course of several weeks, usually with Champ. He could tell there was less tension on the lead line, but never once attempted to bolt or break free. Finally, one particularly warm day, Champ was feeling especially spunky. I was attempting to hold Bella back behind him as he tried to outrun her, when I looked up to see a patch of woods directly in our path. As I continued to struggle controlling the two horses I realized I could sacrifice myself running into the tree line with Bella, or I could let go. I chose to let go. Bella sped into another gear, and Champ followed. We raced all the way back to the barn with Champ in close pursuit, turned in to the paddock, and completed our ride. It was amazing!

A few days later as I prepared to ride, I put the bridle and reins on Bella, and noticed that Champ was waiting for me to connect the lead line to his halter. Rather than connect it this time, I wrapped it around my shoulder, mounted Bella, and led her out. Champ followed us as naturally, as if this was our usual routine. We made our own trail that day, as I wanted this particular ride to be anything but routine. We tracked back and forth across the fields, sometimes circled or retraced our path, and Champ continued to follow. I knew

I'd go immediately to him if he decided to divert from us, but the two horses moved as one. Eventually we made our way into the forest, where he completely transformed. I've never seen my Champ look so youthful, young, and free. He's a quarter horse by breed, but in the woods that day he was a beautiful wild mustang, free as the wind. The way he carried his head, tightened his butt, flattened his back, stretched out his girth—all told the world that he was without a bit, bridle, reins, or lead line and he KNEW it! He was going to show everyone he was free! He would run out in front of us, then cut back behind us and follow, alternating at will. There were some men in the woods cutting down trees, so he spooked a bit, bolting away, but then returned and stepped in right alongside us. We eventually arrived at a stream that Bella and I had jumped over several times in the past, but I had never been able to get heavy-footed Champ to jump it. He'd slow down and plod carefully over until we were past. On this day, though, he saw the stream ahead in his path, and began to trot along with Bella and me. Bella and I jumped it, and I looked back just in time to see Champ gaining momentum and also jumping into it without hesitation! As we moved out of the woods and back onto the open fields, I gave Bella the cue to run, and she took off like lightning. Champ broke into a gallop too, beginning on the other side of the field, and converging to run parallel with Bella. They joined up closely at some point, continuing to run as one. They slowed to a walk as we arrived closer to the barn, and I guided Bella back to the paddock, with Champ following closely behind. They had never looked so proud and healthy as long as I'd known them. It was one of the most exhilarating experiences of my life, and it was all because I trusted my horses and my instincts and let go!

Knowing exactly when to let go involves knowledge, intuition, and instinct, but when emotion enters the mix, it becomes trickier. In personal relationships, whether a friend or a significant other, it's important to know and honor what fuels the other person. When is that person at his or her best, and how can you give love and support? It's a simple concept that should be at the foundation of any relationship, but not always easy to live out.

My last serious relationship began as a blind date and progressed over a couple of years as we spent much of that time getting to know one another at the barn with the horses. She told me that she fell in love with the person I am at the barn, which makes sense, because the barn is where I most feel I am the person God intended me to be. I'm absolutely most aligned spiritually, physically, and emotionally when I'm at the barn with my horses. They fuel me. However, the more time we spent outside the barn in other settings, the more that image crumbled for her. I'm not the same Zen-like person I am at the barn when I'm out in the world. I'm human and regular just like everyone else. I don't enjoy the city as much as the countryside, because of the pace and superficiality of it all. It's just not me.

A couple of years into our relationship, she decided to look for a horse of her own. Unfortunately, that was the beginning of the end. To make a long story short, we didn't agree on how to buy the horse, which horse to buy, what to buy for her horse, who should train him, or how to train him. It exaggerated the faults in our relationship, rather than enhance the strengths. I spent far too much time trying to fix her horse, in order to nurture and fix *us*. She ended up resenting all the time I spent at the barn, when that was the person she fell in love with in the first place. I suppose this theme and story are as old as time. At some point, I had to let go of trying to fix this horse, whom I miss dearly and still worry about to this day. I had to let go of trying to please my girlfriend by compromising who I am and aspire to be. The demise of this relationship and forced letting go of her horse along with it, has given me a very sharp awareness of integrating who I truly am into everything I do, whether that be in business or in my personal life. I aspire to be my most authentic self as often as possible and show up as my best self as much as I can. I realize it's not realistic to be that all the time. Perfection isn't possible or desirable, and that's not what I'm getting at. The idea is to align yourself with who and what you are at your core, then live to that standard wherever you go. Take steps to fuel yourself, find your pace. Find balance in work and with family, friends, and other activities. When you find a piece of the puzzle in life that doesn't align with that balance, and isn't making you or others better, it might just be time to let it go.

INTEGRATION

"Enhance and intensify one's vision of that synthesis of truth and beauty which is the highest and deepest reality."

Ovid

The big idea is about LIVING your brand in every moment to make your business, and your life, better as a whole. Whether your mission is to manufacture and sell the very best widget on the market, give people a wonderful spa experience, or teach in a classroom; it's important to know what you stand for, and embody it. By spelling out the vision, breaking it down to the very roots until it becomes tangible and real, you finally become able to identify that vision in parts, and see yourself living it. The entire process of working the branding and operations models isn't exclusively for the role of growing business—although that's certainly an important element. If that were the case, we at iBG would simply recommend that you eliminate your bottom performing tier of employees to instantly improve your bottom line; but it's about exponentially more than that. Growth happens naturally when you LIVE your brand out in the world, creating more and better believers in what you do! When your company and personal values, vision, mission, language, culture, and accountability align, there are no limits to what you can achieve. Keep refining, defining, and raising the bar! That bar might stand for profit, but it also represents integrity and motivation. It's sometimes difficult to see that with fresh eyes when you're working in the middle of it all on a day-to-day basis.

As we've discussed, change is difficult and often resisted. It's best led by an outside element with an objective viewpoint, willing to work actively side by side in an honest and grounded manner.

Success is realized through:
- Planning
- Branding
- Leading
- Marketing
- Teaching

It's what we love to do. It drives us to continue striving for the same standard for ourselves and our own business! We thrive on implementing change, and embracing new and different cultures. It's travel with a purpose each and every time I enter a new office, home, or even a barn. There is so much yet to learn, inspire, and TO BE inspired by in this world. I get to join people every day in their journey toward self and professional improvement, guiding them towards their best selves, and ultimately leading to success in both business and life. THAT is LIVING my brand!

AFTERWORD

Last Chance Mustang
More Lessons in Horses and Business

I can't overstate how much horses have impacted my life. My experiences with them have evoked many parallels to the business world, and they continue to teach me each time I interact with them. Horse experiences, like life experiences, are ever-changing and challenging. Just when you think you have it figured out, it morphs into an entirely new and unfamiliar situation. Much of the problem lies within the hurts, habits, and hang-ups we (and horses) have acquired and integrated into our daily lives for as long as we can remember. In as much as we can't change the way we sneeze, we can't change our responses to different situations without a very conscious awareness of ourselves, and the dynamic that causes our response. It's possible to learn and change, but often not without the unbiased input of an outside influence like a coach, and concerted effort on our parts. Sometimes we can only hope to adapt, and compensate, to function at our best.

The book *Last Chance Mustang* by Mitchell Bornstein illustrated this so very clearly for me, as so many of Borstein's experiences mirrored my adventures with my own adopted horses Bella, Champ, and Snickers. Last Chance Mustang is the story of Samson, a formerly wild American Mustang captured from the free-roaming herds of Nevada by the Bureau of Land Management. The process by which these horses are driven from their homes and detained has been notoriously documented as abusive, and the conditions in which they are kept after capture, overcrowded and inhumane. Samson's experience was no different. After a helicopter chased him with the rest of the herd for days, he was finally exhausted and frightened enough to be apprehended, and eventually sold. Some mustangs may indeed find wonderful owners willing to work with them to rehabilitate and train them toward a purposeful domesticated existence; but Samson instead fell into a cycle of abuse and futility. The more humans tried to break him through pain and fear, the wilder he became, until horse trainer Mitchell Bornstein became his last chance at any kind of quality domesticated horse life. Mr. Bornstein documented his time with Samson from the time he first met him barricaded in a dank, cement-floored old milking stall, to working through many of his issues, and eventually riding him. Samson would always be wild though and would continue to carry the burden of his many physical and emotional scars.

Bornstein is a horse trainer known for working with horses who had been written off by others as hopeless. He has seen many tough cases over his many years of horse training but admits that Samson was the worst. Samson had survived thus far by living the motto, "Be proud. Never show weakness. Strike first. Never shy from a fight." Samson had injured most living beings—equine or human—that came anywhere near him, but Bornstein felt a connection to Samson, and was compelled to at least try to give him a chance. Samson's survival skills were really just defense mechanisms, serving to protect him from the terror of being captured, and all of the trauma that followed. We all carry some type of defense in place to help us deal with the rigors of daily life or work experiences, and perhaps born from an earlier time in our lives. Sometimes they serve us well, but more often than not, they can impede our success and hold us back from reaching our full potential. Such was the case with Samson and his owner, Amy.

From the beginning, Amy's intentions were noble; save a horse, and give him a comfortable happy home to live out the rest of his days. But Samson came with a reputation, and that reputation—along with aggressive behaviors that threatened everyone on Amy's farm—doomed any chance for a peaceful relationship between Samson and Amy. This same dynamic occurs daily in the work world. How many people go into work fearing a boss, co-worker, or client? Unless you face those fears, and I would argue unless you conquer them, they will continue to act as roadblocks to reaching maximum success in any given situation. Horses are very intuitive to emotions like fear. They pick up on submissive body language or tone of voice. Horses, like many animals, are opportunists. It is strongly entrenched in their DNA that only the strong survive. Step into the stall of an insecure horse and make the wrong moves at the wrong times, and you could reap a serious consequence like a head-butt or kick in the pants. Similarly, fear and insecurity are easily conveyed, or even projected, in the work place. "Fear, it turns out, begets insecurity in both humans and horses." Defense mechanisms kick in, and before you know it, you've talked yourself out of a deal or a promotion. It may not display itself this plainly in a given situation, but as we've discussed earlier, people fear change, and are most comfortable with what they know. Old patterns, dysfunctional as they may be, are preferable to the work and time that change requires. Bornstein wisely says that, "…impatience not only breeds failure, but can just as easily lead to rash decisions and careless actions." There is no shortcut, but the rewards can be great! In Amy's case, she got stuck. For her own safety and the other animals on the farm, she quarantined Samson to a remote concrete stall. No one was brave enough to enter it to clean it out, so it became a physical prison for Samson, and an emotional one for Amy. Fear won out and stunted any forward progress for Amy and Samson. Enter horse trainer, Mitchell Bornstein.

Bornstein goes on to say, "…a domesticated horse expects its handler to be both strong and confident." In the human world, a worker expects his or her leader to be both strong and confident. This doesn't mean egotistical and controlling; rather strong, confident, and *stable*. Strong leadership and guidance (because that's what leading is) requires consistency, follow-through, and accountability in the actions he or she takes. It might require going back to basics to make sure the foundations of an organization are strongly rooted and aligned. There should be processes in place; Standard Operating Procedures by which things are done. Employees will be on-board in following the leader who has created such an environment because confidence begets confidence. Success begets success. So even when there are unknowns, with these structures in place, leaders can behave like they know what they're doing, and all will follow—even when they don't necessarily know what comes next at that given moment! When Bornstein first stepped into Samson's stall, he didn't truly know how Samson would react. The horse could have charged and trampled him. It was one option among many Samson could have chosen in that moment. The experienced horse trainer entered the stall confidently, while still respecting Samson's space. More importantly, he entered it slowly, each movement carefully choreographed to Samson's terrified body language. There are no givens in animal behavior. What works with one horse may or may not work with another, so although there might be patterns and likely outcomes, in the end that horse chooses how to react based on personality and past experiences. Bornstein spent over twenty peaceful minutes in Samson's stall that first meeting before the horse seemingly transformed in an instant, kicking out and nearly laying blows to Borstein's chest. It turns out a helicopter had flown by, and the sound brought back the panic of being chased by a helicopter back in Nevada. It was one of many mysteries yet to be uncovered in the depths of Samson's mind and psyche, and acutely reminded me of my days reading books to Bella in her stall while she learned to tolerate, and finally trust me.

For Samson and his trainer, there was "an understanding premised upon mutual trust, loyalty, and sacrifice" that came to be after many months of hard work. It was a gradual building of credibility based solely upon experiences between the two. In the beginning, Bornstein had to rely on past years of horse training, and the progressions he knew had worked best for specific behaviors. Some of those techniques worked, and some were thrown out the window because Samson was unique! In business when you have a new leader or employee, you need to begin with the foundation and parameters currently in place. You need a starting point. This is our culture; this is how we act. This is our language; this is how we speak. That person becomes fluent in how to act and speak automatically, within and outside of the organization. The operations side will illustrate how things should be *done* down to the most minute details. The model is fluid though, allowing for changes along the way toward continuous improvement. In the very beginning, the guidelines are strict: Stick to the model! Stick to the Standard Operating Procedures! Once familiar, fluent, and experienced, leader and employee will naturally know when to apply strict guidelines and allow exceptions to the rules. It's a nuance that comes from experience, and the freedom of a good system incorporating enhancements. In fact, our best lessons can be learned from a challenging employee or leader just as Mitchell Bornstein became a better horse trainer after working with Samson. Bornstein noted that, "Samson has never made anything easy, has made a point of consistently and constantly challenging my abilities... I have valued and indeed cherished this Mustang's ways, for they taught that a good horseman never stops questioning his methods, improving his skills, and learning new ways." That is the definition of what a leader should embody. Never be complacent, and never get too comfortable!

One example when the rules for Samson were thrown out the door was the time a cantankerous veterinary assistant from the race track, with no love or respect for Samson's past, came to the farm to give Samson his vaccinations. He did not appreciate Bornstein's presence, taking it to mean that he was not capable of controlling this horse on his own (he wasn't) and doing his job. He barged into Samson's stall with a chip on his shoulder and an attitude of aggression and dominance. Samson reacted by instantly and violently kicking both the stall door and veterinary assistant out of his stall and out of his personal space. Samson seemed to instantly realize what he'd done once Bornstein peacefully entered his stall and led him outside for his shots. He was a model citizen and complied with everything asked of him. In this case Bornstein forgave him for the outburst and didn't dole out any consequences. In both horses and business, there are standards to uphold, and accountabilities to satisfy, but there are exceptions to every rule and every standard. If you are not aware of the language by which to comprehend when that exception needs to be made, and don't act accordingly, you can actually end up lowering your standards. In this case, a person with no care for the safety of the horse, and ready to rule by pain and punishment, got what he deserved. Of course, Bornstein had been working with Samson, so people and other animals would be safe around him. But when Samson's safety was threatened, and he acted accordingly in his defense, his behavior was justified. That aggressive veterinary assistant would no longer be allowed on the farm and would not threaten Samson again. In a business world full of complicated human relationships, we sometimes need to tell someone they're wrong. The line between being collaborative and authoritative can be tricky to walk, but necessary to protect integrity of the business and people within it.

Samson's trainer recognized from the beginning that his outbursts were never malicious. They were borne out of fear, and years of pain and trauma. Samson needed to realize that Bornstein was there as his advocate. He would never inflict pain or use fear to accomplish their training goals. I've suffered three concussions and numerous falls while working with my horses. Initially, when I'd fall off and the horse would run back to the barn without me, I would take offense! I finally realized that they were simply going back to their safe place—the barn. In the work environment, the first concern that surfaces when talking about corrections is that people will be hurt, and people will be offended. People take criticism personally. There's a correct way to address remediations. Time, patience, and instruction will lead to a vast array of desired, appropriate responses following a discussion about improvement or change. When you take one-on-one time with any employee at any tier, it's important to take the time to follow up with him or her, and make sure they have a comfort level with the changes you've asked for, and that a new sense of confidence emerges. It comes back to being heard, respected, and safe. You'll find you can push people outside of their comfort zones toward self-improvement and the greater good of the company, and they will embrace it because of the trust established in your professional relationship. In the end, you are a team; partners in the truest sense. A true partnership is reciprocal by nature. One needs to support and fuel the other as needed and vice versa. An unbalanced relationship will have one constantly striving to please the other, and one doling out the tasks and judgment. A leader can't see his or her role to simply please everyone and keep the peace. That might work in the short term, but you won't progress forward as a team. Ultimately, the leader motivates and fuels, and the team rises to the occasion. When you're stuck doing work that doesn't fuel you, you will tend to avoid certain tasks, and induce failure along the way. There has to be something that motivates and fulfills you to be at your best.

Sometimes that motivation falls outside of work. It might be family, a hobby, a sport, or even a horse. Mitchell Bornstein balanced a career as a lawyer with family, friends, a girlfriend, and horse training. When Samson charged into his life, he required a commitment that lasted the better part of two years. Any significant lapse in time between training sessions would result in a lapse of progress, and a need to retrain behaviors already mastered. Samson would regress. With so much of his time and energy spent on and with Samson, Bornstein's neglected girlfriend finally bailed on the relationship. He laments, "With my fortieth birthday just weeks away, unmarried with no children, wanting to be married and have children, I was once again a jockey with no horse. A horse with no jockey… The problem, however, was that I wasn't devastated… In truth, if Jamie were 'the one' then she would have understood." Once again, I can relate. It's sometimes difficult to manage the demands of a job, a relationship, and another life passion. One only has so much energy and focus to give. When it comes to things like relationships, work, and an outside influence like horses, you sometimes figure out that you can't have it all. Balance becomes difficult, and you become mediocre at best. Most of us feel overwhelmed with our responsibilities at one point or another. Many struggle daily, unable to meet high personal and societal demands. Realizing that you sometimes can't have it all isn't necessarily a bad thing. Finding that gray area, that place of compromise, isn't a bad philosophy but it won't make you great. Making a choice to commit to what's most important and pare away the rest optimizes your abilities and your potential in a much less diluted way.

In the end, Samson, with the help of his dedicated trainer, met his owner Amy's demands that he be tamed and ridden in order to remain a resident on the farm. His life depended on it; if they had failed, Samson would likely have been sold and sent to slaughter or used as a bucking horse in some second-string rodeo. Bornstein recalls the day he knew he and Samson would share life-long understanding and friendship. As Bornstein entered his pasture, where Samson always stood facing west as if longing for the wild land of the plains he had lost forever, "On this day Samson rotated around, faced me, and turned his back on the memories and longings that had fueled his survival through his darkest moments. For Samson, it was a simple act that said that he was finally at peace and ready for a new start. For me, it was a monumental act that left me surprisingly touched." Samson turned out to be a "one-man horse" that no one else could ride, so his owner offered him up to Bornstein. Although he loved this horse, he couldn't bring himself to move Samson away from the equine companions he finally accepted as family, and the pasture and barn where he felt comfortable enough to feel at home. But he vowed to come back"...the next week, and the week after that, and month after that. I will never leave you, old boy." Bornstein's dedication to Samson surely grew from all of the time and effort spent together, and it paid off exponentially for both. He likely saved Samson's life, and in turn, Samson gave him the trust and love that he had never given another human being. There hadn't been one deserving of it before. It's interesting that I also have a "one-man horse" in Bella, the mare I spent hours reading to in her stall until she begrudgingly let me into her world. Similarly, when I work with a client and his or her business, I get to know everyone involved very well on several different levels. It might start tentatively, but over time we learn together, we explore strengths and weaknesses, we walk together through change. I relish seeing an organization thrive, in part because of the work we've done together. I found my passion through horses. They fuel me, teach me, balance me, and generally make me a better person. I'm thankful and blessed to take all of that, turn it around, and channel some of that positive energy directly back into my work through iBG. All my experiences to date have led me to where I am in this moment. I'd like to say that horses have made me enlightened and in a peaceful Zen state, but that wouldn't be entirely accurate. They've given me peace enough to say I'm almost where I'm supposed to be, and I can't wait to leap on, and see where the ride takes me in the days, months, and years to come!

ABOUT THE AUTHORS

Michael Armeli is a branding expert with respect to strategic growth, as well as horse enthusiast, and entrepreneur. Michael founded integrated Brand Group (iBG) in 2005. With an international business and marketing background, Michael focuses on closing the gap between business strategy (high level thinking) and living the brand (ground level operations). This gap can create a misguided culture within a business, and an unclear roadmap to growing to its full potential.

Working with all types of businesses and organizations, Michael integrates and aligns core values with operational procedures, partnering with company leaders at all levels of an organization. He believes a brand defines every aspect of an organization and its people. Over the years, Michael built the proprietary process he applies to organizations to help them define how to "LIVE Your Brand" both inside and outside of the company, while creating buy-in from team members and building a positive organizational culture.

Today, executives cannot rely solely on traditional marketing methods for growth. Company leaders are asking for help in achieving growth and financial results by combining clear business strategy with a robust brand and speaking in a compelling voice to the market. iBG continues to grow and expand, serving clients in the Midwest and other regions of the United States.

When not at work with iBG, Michael enjoys time with his beloved dog Sofi, horses Bella and Champ, and working on the farm. Michael is excited to bring the "LIVE Your Brand" message to the world, and encourages you to be your best authentic self both in business and in life!

Amy Oaks brings combined experiences in communications and public speaking, sports business, public relations, sales, and finally as a small business owner, along with years of teaching in the health and fitness field to her current position of "author". She has a previously published Amazon Best Seller to her credit titled *Go Solo! A Savvy Woman's Guide to Transformation & Self-Discovery Through Travel*, co-authored with Jennifer Buchholz. Amy enjoys a good walk, a good book, an occasional paddle-board excursion, and her family. She is blessed with an understanding husband, Jon, two amazing sons Connor and Jordan, and two loving adopted dogs Luigi and Lacy.

Thank you, Michael Armeli, for the honor of writing this book with you, and for teaching me about the deeper intricacies of business operations and branding. I've strived for years to be my authentic self through yoga, my faith, and health and wellness practice, among other things, but now understand that well-defined processes and accountability can make all the difference. I'm thrilled to help bring the "LIVE Your Brand" message to the world with you!

www.ingramcontent.com/pod-product-compliance
Lightning Source LLC
Chambersburg PA
CBHW060610200326
41521CB00007B/731